Down in the Dumps . . . .

What green economy?

Down in the Dumps.....

What green economy?

Marcus J Farmer

authorHOUSE®

AuthorHouse™
1663 Liberty Drive
Bloomington, IN 47403
www.authorhouse.com
Phone: 1-800-839-8640

First published by AuthorHouse   10/05/2011

ISBN: 978-1-4567-9797-3 (sc)
ISBN: 978-1-4567-9798-0 (ebk)

Printed in the United States of America

Any people depicted in stock imagery provided by Thinkstock are models, and such images are being used for illustrative purposes only.
Certain stock imagery © Thinkstock.

This book is printed on acid-free paper.

DEDICATED TO THE OTHER 56

'How many times can a man turn his head pretending he just doesn't see'

Bob Dylan (Blowin' in the wind)

Author's note

One of the hardest things for anyone to accept in life is the feeling of injustice, particularly when the law enforcement agencies that are there to protect you claim they have done a 'thorough' investigation to try and ensure justice prevails. When the door of investigation shuts, when all avenues have been exhausted, and your request for the decision to be reviewed based on fresh evidence has been ignored, there is only one peaceful and civilised response. The only card left for you to play is to write your own truthful account of what happened, backed up with clear evidence. From there, the reader can decide.

Most of the information included in this book is already in the public domain. I have simply pulled it together, along with emails and letters that were sent to me, to form a clear audit trail as the basis of a wider argument. By telling this story, I believe I am acting in the interests of the general public, particularly of those who want to see a thriving green economy that gives Britain millions of genuine, responsible jobs for the future. I also firmly believe that every man has the right to defend his livelihood and that of his employees, and must do everything he can to protect himself from threats beyond his control. The same man must also do everything in his power to restore a reputation tarnished by those in an official capacity who have left him to perish on an issue that is actually very straight forward.

On Thursday 6 May 2010, I stood as an independent candidate at the UK general election. On that day, I officially became a politician in a land where it is my democratic right to stand up and be counted for what I believe in. In order to make a sound political point and promote a civilised debate, there should always be a full explanation of the situation and at least one good example that illustrates your case. That is what you will find in this book.

It is my belief that the politics promoted in this book are the politics of the future that can rescue our ailing economy and offer hope and optimism to the next generation.

Marcus Farmer
Managing Director, STE Waste

Introduction

When you are emotionally involved in a situation, you are unlikely to do it justice when writing about it unless you take enough time to reflect and objectively analyse all the main points. This is a story that had to be written with a clear, analytical and level head, and not by someone angry, dejected and disillusioned. Between January and March 2011, I put this whole situation to one side. I picked it up again in mid April when a letter and key piece of official information arrived out of the blue, raising more questions than answers about those in charge of the investigation.

This story is about my own personal struggle within the fledgling green economy. I am seeking to expose the concept of plausible deniability, the UK's obsession with ticking boxes in the name of certification, the lack of green legislation and the absence of clear government environmental policy—all of which make it almost impossible for the authorities to ensure fair play. The book also looks at the spin placed on the environment by our politicians, and delves into the topical question of the use of defamation law to keep people quiet when they are clearly looking to hold a responsible debate in the interests of the general public.

When writing this book I have used the scientific principles of evaluating evidence, coupled with the concepts of free enquiry and criticism—surely the hallmark of any progressive, democratic society. On a personal level, I have also written the book to restore my own reputation as a person who is not looking to cause trouble, but who simply wants to put right an industry that is in danger of seriously damaging our environment for future generations. I hope this book will be received as a 'responsible publication on a matter of public interest' and not as one 'actuated by malice'.

What you are about to read is my version of a UK Trading Standards investigation based on a complaint that I made. I am aiming to show just how far we need to go to give our green economy any chance of long term success. I genuinely believe that, due to a lack of investigative resources, understanding and the possibility of embarrassing those involved, my complaint was kept out of the public domain, thereby silencing the only man who was shouting.

Regrettably, the only civilised response now open to me is to go public with my complaint because no one in an official position of authority will listen to what I have to say. It is my sincere hope that this book will promote a healthy debate on the future of the UK's green economy.

The green economy and one part in particular

There are people better qualified than me to define the green economy in academic, technical and economic terms. This is my own simple definition for the purpose of this book.

'The green economy is probably our best opportunity for getting our nation out of the economic mess it currently finds itself in. If promoted and defended correctly, it could guarantee freedom and democracy for future generations through self sufficiency and sustainability.

Any successful economy is built around consumer confidence. So it stands to reason that, if a green economy is to emerge, consumers must have confidence in its products and services. Likewise, the people and organisations that are providing genuine green products and services must be confident that they will be protected against offerings that are mere marketing illusions. Unless consumers and providers trust and believe in what they are buying and selling, then sadly, the whole green concept falls apart and becomes yet another missed opportunity for the UK.'

I think it is safe to say that the vast majority of politicians have now jumped on the environmental band wagon and are happy to promote 'green' as a positive concept. In theory, and with enterprise, innovation and ingenuity based on free market principles, the green economy will create millions of jobs as new ethical products, ideas and services enter the consumer market. Everything will be cleaner and fresher as we change the way we live and protect our planet at the same time. Our over-reliance on the service sector and the risk this presents to our domestic economy will be reduced by a new wave of high tech production and traditional agrarian management techniques, which will create morally-responsible wealth on an unprecedented scale. As we move closer to becoming a self sufficient country, the future of our freedom and democracy will be secured.

With confidence, international investment houses will put big money into research and development, making fossil fuels redundant as we start reducing, reusing and recycling—and reclaiming the feel good factor at the same time. New environmental household brand names will appear that we can all invest in, reaping proud dividends along the way. Everything will point to a positive future for the next generation as we all strive for a better environment where the role of science takes centre stage. The green pound will be the new currency that we all spend and save, and consumer confidence will be secured by our trust in these new products and services.

Theoretically, the green economy has huge potential for creating the jobs of the future. This is why there is now a general consensus amongst all British political parties that this is where the future lies. However, one of this book's main arguments is that, although our politicians might play the green card, very few of them actually understand it. I will argue that, without clearly defined policy in the form of legislation and protection for genuine companies, there is actually no chance of creating a flourishing green economy. The key to long term success for any long term political ideology lies in the foundations laid down in the complex planning stage. I believe that, currently, the green economy has no firm foundations due to a severe lack of planning by the UK government. For a catalyst to happen, our politicians need to understand this. The green economy will not just emerge from nowhere and in the short term, the lack of rules, regulations and policies may actually cause it to fail.

Another of the book's key arguments is that we need to study the science of how humans react with their environment if new ideas are to have any chance of fruition. Without free enquiry and the ability to criticise without fear of expensive legal retribution, the massive opportunities offered by the green economy have little chance of ever picking up speed. In fact, responsible and positive criticism of anything that is based in science is essential if we are to make progress.

This all started as a local spat between two waste companies (my own in Manchester and the other in Liverpool), a situation which should have been dealt with swiftly by the authorities. Instead, in the space of twelve months during 2010, it grew into an issue to which I am now prepared to dedicate the rest of my working life: sound environmental practice.

The waste industry

If you asked most British people to name words relating to the environment, my guess is that 'recycling' would be one of the most popular answers. Although many political commentators criticise the New Labour years, there is no doubt that they successfully promoted recycling as a key part of their environmental strategy, to the extent that most people now separate their domestic waste into the various streams (cardboard, glass and so on).

However, although we have set and often exceeded certain targets, the UK still lacks a national strategic waste policy that clearly sets out how we manage our waste resources. As a result, almost every council in the country has a different approach to managing waste. Some have blue bins for waste paper whereas others have red. Some mix the various waste streams and tell us it gets sorted elsewhere, whilst others are committed to turning waste into energy and burn the lot. (This so-called 'dash for ash' is a huge political topic, and the final chapter of this book discusses whether it should ever be classed as a green solution when the reality is that burning waste destroys resources that could otherwise be reused to generate wealth within the economy. The fact that much of the processing of UK waste for energy takes place after it has been transported by ship to Scandanavia only adds to the scientific debate of what is environmental and what is not).

Because the UK's waste industry has no national strategic policy, it is totally lacking in transparency and agreed method. The only constant is the need for every commercial player to show its green credentials to their target market. As long as companies promote the correct image and say the right things then the people and organisations that need to tick their own environmental boxes are likely to use their services. Everyone who collects and processes waste knows this. As a result, it is now more important than ever before that waste industry players actively market their recycling results to their target audiences to boost their perceived profile within the sector. Unsurprisingly, a positive environmental perception is directly proportional to higher profits, client inertia and market share. For example, a 95% recycling claim, if it was correct, would therefore, quite rightly, always win the quote against one of just 65% and would by definition be more likely to make money in the waste sector.

On top of this, environmental legislation now obliges larger companies and organisations to make an annual corporate and social responsibility statement as part of their financial reporting. To make green claims, these companies therefore need to use suppliers that can tick the right environmental boxes. A key part of the corporate and social responsibility statement relates to waste management and, in particular, recycling commitments. So clearly it is in a company's interests to choose a waste management supplier that has a good recycling record. In other words, recycling is a major factor in a company's economic behaviour when selecting a waste provider. For anyone or any organisation to dispute this is simply absurd. Here are two examples which provide evidence that recycling is clearly linked to economic behaviour. The first is a press release issued by Peel Land & Property:

Marcus J Farmer

'PRESS RELEASE

21ˢᵗ June 2010

Peel Achieve 86.4% Recycling Rate

Peel Land & Property has achieved an incredible 86.4% recycling rate across its managed sites in the North West.

Of all the waste created by tenants at Peel managed sites across the North West, an average of 86.4% of it has been recycled in the first quarter of 2010. At some sites in the North West, an astounding 94.3% of the waste is being recycled.

The type of waste produced determines how it will be recycled. General waste can go through a waste-to-energy process in order to produce fuel/energy whereas paper and card waste will go to a materials recycling facility. At this facility, the waste is separated depending on the type of waste, and paper and card can be recycled to produce fibre.

B&M Waste Services Ltd, who provide the service, transport selected waste material to a processing plant in Merseyside. The plant has developed a range of patented technologies to recover and recycle up to 95% of the waste delivered to it. The process recovers valuable commodities and produces a range of sustainable fuels for the production of green heat energy, renewable electricity and low carbon road transport fuels.

The recycling performance of each Peel managed site is determined by calculating the weight of unrecyclable residue left at the end of the process as a proportion of the waste material delivered to the plant. This non-recyclable residue is a very small proportion of the initial material, and due to its inert nature has no impact on greenhouse gas generation.

Paul Chappels, Head of Investment at Peel said: "We are very pleased to receive an average recycle rate of 86.4% as much of the remaining waste has very little impact on the environment. Peel's commitment to recycling is part of a wider strategy that saw Peel recently awarded the Carbon Trust Standard.'

Vicki Hulse, Marketing Manager at B&M Waste Services Ltd said, 'We are pleased to take this opportunity to work in partnership with Peel Land & Property. Together we now utilise the very latest technologies to successfully achieve a very high recycling rate and minimal landfill.'

Notes to Editors

Peel Land & Property comprises a UK property investment and land portfolio of 836,000 sq m (9 million sq.ft) of investment property and over 11,000 hectares (25,000 acres) of land as well as overseas investments in Bermuda, the Bahamas and Spain. With a track record for quality and regeneration, high profile developments encompass The Trafford Centre, MediaCityUK, Gloucester Quays and the visionary Liverpool and Wirral Waters £10 billion regeneration schemes.

Peel Land & Property is a division of The Peel Group which is a leading infrastructure, transport and real estate investment company in the UK with assets owned and under management approaching £6 billion.'

The '*processing plant*' referred to in the fourth paragraph of the press release is Orchid Environmental in Huyton, Liverpool. Its performance is open for anyone to analyse under the Freedom of Information Act. In the first quarter of 2010, according to the waste returns that Orchid lodged with the Environment Agency, 728.79 tonnes out of 9,485.52 tonnes of waste removed from the Huyton site was recycled. That equates to a recycling rate of just 7.68%. It would therefore appear that Peel, one of the UK's leading land and property companies, is making environmental claims that are indeed incredible—but which also need to be analysed and carefully questioned.

In July 2011, the Orchid plant in Liverpool closed. The site had become financially unviable because most of the waste material taken there wasn't suitable for recycling or producing sustainable fuels. Recovering valuable commodities would certainly have been very difficult because the waste would already have been shredded during the first process of Orchid's waste management method.

The second example is an email that my company receives each month from a top four UK waste player in our capacity as sub contractor. This confirms both the importance of recycling and the expectations placed on waste services suppliers within the industry. It also shows the significance of recycling certification and reports to the waste producer who has important environmental boxes to tick.

'Hi Marcus

Please could we have your recycling figures for the month of February.

OVERALL RECYCLING PERCENTAGE			
Total Tonnage processed through facility	Total Tonnage to Landfill	Total Tonnage Recycled	Recycling %

If your general waste is taken to a separate facility, please could the table below be completed.

GENERAL WASTE		
Container Type	Type of Facility the waste is taken to	Recovery percentage

Please could this information be sent to me at **dutyofcare@biffa.co.uk** by the **25th March**.

Why do we need this information?

As environmental policy and corporate responsibility continue to grow in importance, many of our customers are becoming increasingly focused on the amount of their waste which is recycled or landfilled and therefore, our customers have a requirement to know what percentage of waste your facility recycles. Each month a report is produced which informs our customers of how much of their waste has been recycled, so it is extremely important to us that we can gather this information together as quickly as possible to ensure that the report is completely accurate.

Kind regards,
Biffa.'

For waste management companies, it therefore stands to reason that the better their recycling performance, the higher the chances that they will keep their clients and sell their services to other organisations who like what they hear.

However, there is a major problem with the concept of filling in and ticking boxes: the temptation to exaggerate your claims and give your company an unfair advantage over others. The email from Biffa might be straightforward and a genuine request for information but it relies completely on trust. So it is quite easy for a cynic to argue that it is a direct request to 'Tell us what we want to hear so we can tick our boxes and report back to our clients'. And because the audit trail stops at the boxes that are ticked, this paves the way to plausible deniability for everyone who receives the information.

The sad truth about the waste industry is that there are those who play by the book and those who don't. Unfortunately, this means it is almost impossible for a genuinely green-minded company to be able to compete as the information provided by best environmental practice doesn't give a quick fix to the problem of ticking boxes. Client demand for high recycling percentages in an industry littered with brokers, middlemen and underhand salespeople means that the recycling certificate, a mere piece of paper, is frequently worth more than the service itself.

In January 2010, as Managing Director of STE Waste in Manchester, I had a commercial dilemma which meant I had to choose one of three options:

1. Accept the situation as part of the industry and eventually go out of business.
2. Go with the status quo and start supplying our own dubious recycling reports in order to tick our clients' environmental boxes and be able to compete in the marketplace.
3. Challenge the status quo and campaign for positive change by reporting the issue to the organisations and law enforcement agencies that are there to promote fair green trading. Also, lobby my local MP who campaigns vociferously on the issue of environmental concerns.

I chose option 3 as I felt this was the morally-responsible way to proceed in the long term and because I had faith in all those employed to protect the green economy. I didn't know it at the time, but I was about to enter a minefield.

This is the story of that minefield.

Chapter 1

An Honest Opinion

'I think we ought always to entertain our opinions with some measure of doubt. I shouldn't wish people dogmatically to believe any philosophy, not even mine.'
Bertrand Russell
(British author, mathematician and philosopher [1872-1970])

To set the scene for this story, I need to go back to 1993. After finishing university and travelling the world for a year or so, the only graduate job I could find in a slow economic climate was training as a chartered accountant. It wasn't long before I decided that analysing other people's figures and following endless audit trails wasn't the job for me. So, like many people in the same position, I decided to follow my dream and start my own business. At 24 years old I had very little money, but I had a good understanding of figures and a degree in Management Science & Marketing. The Prince's Business Youth Trust was handing out grants and cheap loans at the time and you could get £50 a week on top if you could convince the government you had entrepreneurial spirit. I wrote a business plan and was lucky enough to secure a £1,500 grant as well as a £1,000 loan. Together with £400 of my own money, I was able to buy an old van at auction and have a few thousand promotional leaflets made.

My business plan hinged on the basic principle that everything tangible has a second life or in other words, on finding a secondary trading market for items that other people no longer want or need. Having worked in an accountant's office for two years where many of the old guard still didn't use computers, I saw firsthand just how much paper ended up in the general waste bin, destined for the tip. You didn't need to be a genius to realise that the recycling industry had a huge future, where a sophisticated marketing approach would soon turn this traditionally lower class service into one for the educated middle classes. Swampy and his eco warriors were starting to get huge press coverage, and the environment was gathering momentum as a key political card. Within the waste industry, a market was suddenly opening where people could be educated away from the 'throw away' society and steered towards one that could trade its waste resources on the international commodity markets.

STE Waste, an acronym for Save The Environment Waste, was born on 4 November 1994. For the next 12 years, the company twisted and turned as its founder tried out many different entrepreneurial avenues. Like many people, I made a small fortune from buying and selling houses as New Labour created the economic property bubble that we are now all paying the price for. Having called the top of the market in 2006, I found myself in an enviable position where nothing could go wrong. I had come a long way on my journey—but like many in this position, I had also become blasé about my success.

I started to look for the next best thing to invest in and almost immediately, something took my interest. A quick analysis of one of STE Waste's clients, Monsoon, showed that they were undervalued on the stock market. Monsoon is a high street retailer that was at the forefront of the then fashion trends for long peasant style dresses and hippy jewellery. My wife was wearing their clothes and so were my daughters—and so were everyone else's wives and daughters. I spent a day driving around all their shops in the North West, looking at their waste bins. At the end of the day, I had reached an economic conclusion: that the rubbish created by a retailer is directly proportional to their profitability.

At the time, a friend of mine was trading shares and seemed to be doing well, so I asked him to introduce me to his stockbroker. I bought a few hundred thousand Monsoon shares at £1 each and saw them rise to £2 within six months. My call had been exactly right and once again I felt nothing could go wrong. But within a year, I was officially a self-confessed gambler, a curse that comes to so many entrepreneurs who overstep the line between informed investor and fool. I had lost all my fortune and more. And like a game of snakes and ladders, I was right back where I started. The two big trades that had taken me down were in the online gambling sector and the debt sector both of which had turned out to be sophisticated business model illusions to entice investors. You can read as many business text books as you like but it is only when you get a 'right good kick in the balls' that you actually learn anything. The big lesson here was to question everything and never take anything at face value.

Most people feel depressed when they lose all their money, but I firmly believe that one's character is only truly tested at times of adversity. After the initial anger at my stupidity had died down, I realised the only person who could get me out of this mess was me. Although I had lost my personal fortune, I still had STE Waste which, although neglected, still provided me with a decent income.

The positive side of my experience was that I learned to value the things I had previously taken for granted. Soon, I realised that if I stuck to doing one thing well instead of having fingers in different pies, I could use my experience to build an environmental brand that would be the envy of many. The brand would focus initially on waste and the principle would be the same as my original business plan: that everything tangible has a second life. For the purposes of this book, I will now refer to this principle as **real recycling**.

The best definition of real recycling can be found on the official political lobby website, 'Campaign for real recycling' (www.realrecycling.org.uk):

Recycle:
1. to pass through a cycle again
2. to use again and again
(Collins Concise English Dictionary)

Real Recycling is about maximising the economic, environmental and social benefits of recycling for everyone, from local council tax payers to the national and global reprocessing industries.

Commingled collection systems that gather a range of different materials in one bag or bin and then compact them frequently create materials unsuitable for reprocessing.

'Source separated' collection systems, however, produce materials that can be reprocessed, usually in the UK, creating value and benefits for everyone.

The needs of the re-processor should be central to the design of any collection system. Source separated collection systems separate materials as much as possible before they arrive at the local recycling depot ready for sale to a reprocessor. As Mal Williams of the Wales Community Recycling Network puts it; 'The first thing we as collectors did was go and find a market for the materials we were planning to collect. We asked the reprocessors what they wanted and designed our collection system from that starting point.'

In practice this means residents have one or more separate boxes for different 'dry' recyclable materials and another for 'wet' materials such as kitchen waste. These materials are then collected in a way that maintains this separation, usually by placing the materials into different containers on the collection vehicle.

UK reprocessors of paper and glass, clothes and aluminum prefer (and often pay higher prices for) source separated materials.

The improved price for materials collected can be used to offset collection costs.

The Campaign for Real Recycling wants local authorities to ensure reprocessors receive their materials in the same condition as when the householder dropped them into the recycling box in their kitchen.

 Six reasons why source separated is best

 Some problems with commingled collections

"Making the most of our waste resources"

In my opinion, real recycling is the only method of waste management that can guarantee a pure waste commodity that can be traded on the world markets. Any other method leads to contamination. To see its value, you only have to ask why councils in England bother to separate waste if they could get the same results from an easier method involving 'chucking it all in the same bin'.

As predicted back in 1994, the UK's waste industry had by 2006 become a sophisticated marketing machine for environmental concerns. Using green credentials to promote sales, one waste player, Bagnall and Morris (B&M), virtually cornered the general waste collection market in the city of Manchester between the start of 2006 and the end of March 2010. On top of its meteoric rise, B&M, which operated out of Bromborough (60 miles away from Manchester) also claimed to be one of Manchester's many environmental champions. A quick assessment of their business model soon put them on my radar as an organisation whose collection techniques and recycling claims did not stack up.

The situation became even clearer when I had a sales meeting with a major facilities management company in Manchester, where a friend of mine was an associate director and was swiftly moving up the corporate ladder. He kindly arranged for me to meet with the lady who managed all their buildings in Manchester. At the time of our meeting, the company's waste management supplier was B&M.

The meeting went very well, but there was a stumbling block around the levels of recycling being quoted. In terms of environmental reporting, the company could not be expected to go backwards from their current level if they chose to appoint STE Waste. But alarm bells started ringing when the lady mentioned a recycling rate of 95%—a level we couldn't possibly match.

She described their recycling method as 'chucking everything in the same bin', after which the waste would be collected and driven 60 miles to Bromborough for manual sorting and recycling. I told her this had to be wrong—what waste company would drive a 30 tonne truck 60 miles to Manchester, collect a load of rubbish and then drive it back to Bromborough? The lady replied that she had been to the materials recycling facility in Bromborough and seen it in action, and the company had a certificate saying their waste went there, so it must be true.

In the end our meeting came to nothing, but I decided to do some investigating. Although I am STE Waste's Managing Director, I also cover for my drivers when they take holidays. I thought I knew exactly where this company tipped their waste, so one day I took the trouble to watch them and follow one of their trucks to its final destination.

That morning, I fuelled up my own waste vehicle in anticipation of a long drive at the end of the day. Following someone else in the waste industry in your own waste truck in a densely built up area might sound stupid, but it is actually very easy to park up three hundred yards behind and make it look like you are doing the same as them.

As I watched their operatives, the company's method of disposal became clear. There was no evidence of rubbish being sorted at source to make their recycling claims even remotely possible. More often than not, the bins labelled as 'Cardboard Waste' were just thrown in the truck with the general rubbish. But what bothered me most was that a number of huge office buildings would be serviced before the trucks visited the Chinatown area, after which all the take away and restaurant food waste would be mixed in. For this method to work and produce a recycling rate of 95% there would have to be a machine involved that would sort the waste into its various commodity types. There would also have to be an extremely powerful washing and drying process that would protect the waste commodities from contamination. As I have always kept up to speed on developments in waste industry machinery, I knew this type of equipment did not exist and even if it did the energy used to process the waste would almost certainly outweigh any environmental benefits.

As expected, the truck did not go anywhere near Bromborough. Instead, it went to a waste tip in Trafford Park, Manchester called Colliers. Colliers, as we are about to see, carried out no recycling at all at that time and, in fact, didn't even have the facilities to do so.

I now need to introduce waste return information, which anyone may access through the Freedom of Information Act. Waste returns give details of what is received at waste treatment sites, the waste's origin and what happens when it leaves the site. Colliers' waste return for the October to December 2009 period, shown below, is pretty clear and easy to understand as 100% of the waste removed from this site goes to landfill. (All the waste returns in this book are reproduced with the kind permission of the Environment Agency).

Environment Agency

Waste Return

Environmental Protection Act 1990
Pollution Prevention and Control Act 1999

Date of issue:	* Use this form to tell us the type and quantity of controlled waste you have processed at each facility on your site over the last quarter.
	* Please read through the whole form and guidance notes before you start filling anything in.
When completed please E-Mail to:	
monitoring.east@environment-agency.gov.uk	* Please e-mail the completed form back to us within 28 days of the end of the return period to the address on the left.

1 Return Period		**Landfill Sites Only**
Period name:	Year	
Qtr Oct-Dec	2009	**2.5 Remaining void space covered by licence**

2 Operator and site details

	Landfill Sites Only
Site Operator	**2.6 Was the site fully surveyed in the past 12 months?**
COLLIER INDUSTRIAL WASTE LTD	___ if no go to question 2.7 Date Surveyed ___
PPC Permit or WM Licence no.	*How was the void space calculated?*
50496	
Site name	
COLLIER INDUSTRIAL WASTE LTD	**2.7 How have you estimated the remaining void space?**
Site Address	*For example visually or other method*
TREATMENT PLANT	
NASH ROAD	
TRAFFORD PARK	
MANCHESTER	**2.8 Remaining life of site (Years)**
Post Code: M17 1SX	
	Now go to sections 3 and 4 (waste received/removed from site)

2.2 Type of facility

A17 - Physico-Chemical Treatment Facility

2.3 Was a weighbridge used?

	Yes	
Percentage weighed	100	%

2.5 If you are not operating a landfill go to section 3

5 Declaration

I certify that the information in this return is correct to the best of my knowledge and belief.

Name	D M WISHART
Position	CTOC
Phone	7885183574 Date 27/01/2010

6 Disclosure and data protection

The information you provide will be used by the Environment Agency to enable it to fulfil its regulatory and waste management planning responsibilities.
For full information on how the data in this form will be used please see the waste return guidance notes.

WASTE RECEIVED ON SITE

Running total (Amount)	20,599.00

Origin	EWC Waste Code	State	Amount	Units	Additional info					
					final disposal	Used on site	Hazardous	From another facility	Bio'able Municipal	Other Bio'able
Trafford	010413	Sludge	29	Tonnes	No	No	No		No	
Trafford	020603	Liquid	19	Tonnes	No	No	No		No	
Trafford	070212	Solid	17	Tonnes	No	No	No		No	
Trafford	070213	Liquid	43	Tonnes	No	No	No		No	
Trafford	080112	Solid	1	Tonnes	No	No	No		No	
Trafford	080114	Solid	27	Tonnes	No	No	No		No	
Trafford	080120	Sludge	9	Tonnes	No	No	No		No	
Trafford	080410	Sludge	81	Tonnes	No	No	No		No	
Trafford	080416	Solid	10	Tonnes	No	No	No		No	
Trafford	150203	Solid	131	Tonnes	No	No	No		No	
Trafford	160304	Solid	44	Tonnes	No	No	No		No	
Trafford	160306	Sludge	1703	Tonnes	No	No	No		No	
Trafford	161002	Liquid	629	Tonnes	No	No	No		No	
Trafford	161004	Sludge	1	Tonnes	No	No	No		No	
Trafford	170302	Sludge	61	Tonnes	No	No	No		No	
Trafford	190203	Solid	1058	Tonnes	No	No	No		No	
Trafford	190206	Solid	580	Tonnes	No	No	No		No	
Trafford	190703	Liquid	1312	Tonnes	No	No	No		No	
Trafford	190814	Sludge	20	Tonnes	No	No	No		No	
Trafford	200125	Sludge	12	Tonnes	No	No	No		No	
Trafford	200301	Solid	12849	Tonnes	No	No	No		No	
Trafford	010505	Sludge	269	Tonnes	Yes	No	Yes		No	
Trafford	060102	Solid	48	Tonnes	No	No	Yes		No	
Trafford	060104	Sludge	43	Tonnes	No	No	Yes		No	
Trafford	060204	Liquid	230	Tonnes	No	No	Yes		No	
Trafford	060205	Solid	562	Tonnes	No	No	Yes		No	
Trafford	061002	Sludge	4	Tonnes	No	No	Yes		No	
Trafford	080111	Solid	15	Tonnes	No	No	Yes		No	
Trafford	110106	Liquid	23	Tonnes	No	No	Yes		No	
Trafford	110109	Sludge	39	Tonnes	No	No	Yes		No	
Trafford	150110	Solid	99	Tonnes	No	No	Yes		No	
Trafford	160305	Solid	19	Tonnes	No	No	Yes		No	
Trafford	160708	Sludge	24	Tonnes	No	No	Yes		No	
Trafford	160709	Sludge	31	Tonnes	No	No	Yes		No	
Trafford	190205	Solid	517	Tonnes	No	No	Yes		No	
Trafford	200127	Solid	40	Tonnes	No	No	Yes		No	

WASTE REMOVED FROM SITE

Running total (Amount)	19,698.00

Destination	EWC Waste Code	State	Amount	Units	Hazardous	Destination Facility Type
Cheshire	190203	Solid	19,698.00	Tonnes	No	3 - Landfill

7

I also received written confirmation from the Environment Agency that there were no recycling facilities at Colliers. On 4 February 2010 at 14.22, Sally Dennison from the Environment Agency emailed me to say: *'I can confirm that there are indeed no picking belts at Colliers waste treatment facility in Trafford Park.'* In other words, there were no recycling facilities at Colliers at that time, and all the waste delivered there ended up in landfill sites as shown on the waste return.

Despite this evidence, I was willing to give B&M the benefit of the doubt—perhaps their main plant had broken down and using Colliers was just a contingency plan for that one day. I asked my own drivers, who were constantly using the tips in Trafford Park, to keep an eye out for B&M on their travels. Word soon came back that their activity in and around two commercial tips was 'ubiquitous'. As I already suspected, this suggested B&M was doing very little recycling. But at the same time, B&M was giving environmental certificates claiming 95% recycling rates to international facilities management companies who were managing the corporate responsibility requirements of some of Manchester's biggest household names.

For the city of Manchester this was, it seemed, politically toxic. Basically, a waste company from Bromborough, near Liverpool, appeared to be creating a green marketing illusion for the paying tenants who drive the city of Manchester. But in reality, based on observational evidence, it looked like they were tipping all the waste less than a mile away from Manchester United's football ground and into two sites that did almost no recycling whatsoever.

STE Waste did not use Colliers waste transfer station but used a nearby site, Viridor, to dispose of residue waste that could not be recycled using the real recycling technique. Viridor is the waste arm of the FTSE 100 Company Pennon and in 2009, their plant in Trafford Park was very basic with no picking belts for commercial waste. As well as using Colliers, B&M also used Viridor, tipping large amounts of rubbish into the very same place as us and making it impossible for their claims about the use of this site to be any different from ours.

In June 2010, as part of my complaint, I put a direct question to Viridor's Plant Manager. I asked how much of the estimated 400 tonnes a week (circa 20,000 tonnes per annum) tipped by B&M at their site was actually recycled. Viridor declined to answer my question on the basis of commercial confidentiality. I respected this and decided to ask the same question in a different way.

On 8 June 2010 at 07.52 I sent Viridor's Plant Manager the following email:

> *'Hi*
>
> *We have been asked to construct a recycling report by one of our clients for their ISO 14001 environmental statement.*
>
> *My assumption is that none of our waste deposited at your tip was recycled'.*

The same day the Plant Manager replied at 09.35 with this email:

'Hi Marcus

You are correct with your assumption that most of your waste will have been landfilled. We did however recycle small quantities (typically 3—10%) of our commercial waste stream. Hope this helps with your report.'

This email proves that the waste B&M deposited at Viridor's Trafford Park depot was almost all sent to landfill. As they tipped in exactly the same commercial waste pile as we did, this is a fair assumption.

Each time STE Waste went head to head with B&M in trying to sell the virtues of real recycling, the door was closed to us because we could not possibly match the recycling rate being claimed by the market leader. One facilities manager in Manchester even told one of my colleagues to 'sharpen his pencil' as our estimate of '*possibly recycling 70%, if certain segregation methods were used*', was so far out. The real recycling method we were promoting was quite simply inconvenient and less efficient than their current supplier's recycling rates. How could this be?

By summer 2009, my dream of creating a local environmental brand was in tatters. STE Waste just could not compete for any of the larger jobs in Manchester that were controlled by the facilities management companies, and our own client base was quite literally a 'sitting duck' for B&M's salesforce. The straw that broke the camel's back came when our largest client told us that a very competitive quote with impressive recycling rates had landed on her desk. I had known the lady for years, so she agreed to a meeting to discuss the quote. In the end, she said she was actually very sceptical of what the senior B&M sales representative, Wendy Mitchell, had been claiming.

The time had now come for me to (reluctantly) start involving the press. I had a chat with a journalist from the Manchester-based *Crains* business magazine and the story hit the front page on 3 August 2009. *Crains*, which has since folded, was then highly respected within Manchester business circles. However, although the story was exactly where it needed to be, *Crains* could not mention who they were referring to because of the UK's strong defamation laws. I needed the splash to gather momentum and that was only going to happen if I bought into the *Crains* business model, which was built on selling advertising space. By taking out a £15,000, 25 week advertising slot I basically bought STE Waste access to a quality journalist. But the fact remained that, quite rightly, most quality journalists are very reluctant to accuse anyone publically without the backup of a report from a regulatory body that has investigated the case.

I finally made my decision to report B&M to the authorities when STE Waste received a letter from ISS, the facilities management company employed by the government owned Royal bank of Scotland, at the beginning of January 2010. They were moving the bank's waste management contracts to B&M because of '. . . *client pressure to provide a more environmentally friendly way of waste disposal . . . . this in no way reflects the service provided by yourselves*'.

B&M had just taken its first major slice of my business: about £45,000 of crème de la crème waste work in Manchester. And they had won the right to service the Royal Bank of Scotland because of their 'superior environmental operations'. Again, this is clear evidence that recycling and environmental performance statistics are strongly linked to economic behaviour when a company appoints a waste management supplier. In total, between January 2010 and July 2011, B&M took almost £60,000 worth of work off STE Waste. And this doesn't include all the pointless times we were asked to quote for jobs that, in hindsight, we had no chance of ever getting.

For the first part of January 2010, I collated evidence before taking my findings to the various law enforcement agencies. We followed B&M's trucks for a few weeks, taking pictures and filming video in and around Manchester. Once again, the evidence confirmed that their environmental claims were misleading. My sales team also called the facilities management company for each building that B&M serviced, and each time they were told that the recycling rate was around 95%. It soon became apparent that B&M had cornered at least two thirds of Manchester's commercial waste market.

A major stumbling block was that I did not have a copy of a B&M recycling certificate showing the 95% claim. Without an example certificate as evidence, my complaint would be worthless. And having carefully researched the law surrounding Trading Standards investigations, I knew that for a certificate to be considered as evidence, it had to be handed to me by a representative of the organisation.

At this point, my Business Development Manager noticed that one of the buildings serviced by B&M was occupied by The Manchester Evening News (MEN), owned at the time by the Guardian Media Group. I called in a favour from a PR agent who had good connections at the newspaper and told her I had a big story that needed investigating. She kindly put me in touch with her contact who passed the lead on to a young journalist at MEN. Although he was hungry to get hold of the next big splash, it was always at the back of my mind that it was unlikely he would ever get authorisation to print this story given the Guardian Media Group's 'Liberal Left' and politically correct take on the environment and associated matters.

The journalist and I met at the MEN building and I asked him to get hold of the building recycling certificate from the site building manager so I could explain the issue in detail. At the end of the meeting, he said I could keep the certificate because it was '*hardly confidential*' if everyone else in Manchester had one. Bingo!

For copyright reasons, the certificate can't be reproduced here, but it showed a recycling rate of 94.54% for the July to September 2009 period. It was made out to the landlord of the MEN building (ironically, this is a company called Hansainvest that is based in Hamburg, Germany—probably the world's greenest country), care of their international facilities management company, Jones Lang Lasalle. The certificate is very similar to one shown later in this book that was released under the Freedom of Information Act, except the MEN certificate included a nice little pie chart showing the various recycling percentages, including the fact that 31% of the claim was made up of the refuse-derived fuel technique otherwise known as burning. It clearly referred to the B&M waste station in Bromborough and included references to the Environment Agency and ISO 14001 for authenticity purposes.

I now had all the evidence to complete the audit trail in my own mind, and I also felt I had enough information to go to the relevant government bodies employed to protect the environment. First, I informed Trading Standards and then, out of courtesy, I told Jones Lang Lasalle that they were going to be a key part of a Trading Standards investigation into Manchester's waste industry. Straightaway, this caused uproar in their ranks and I received a call from one of their National Directors, a particularly assertive lady who was adamant that the waste from the MEN building went all the way from Manchester to Bromborough to be sorted and recycled.

The next night, I received a phone call from Mr Ken Curtis, the owner of B&M. The conversation went on for around half an hour and various things were said that are irrelevant to the purpose of this book. But what he did say was that the Viridor and Colliers waste tips would back up his recycling claims. I have since asked for evidence of this, but my request was declined due to the 'sensitive and confidential' nature of this information.

It soon became obvious that this was always going to be a tale of denial, despite all the evidence. So I started to look at opportunities which would make it clear that both my complaint and my stand were firm. And with the general election just around the corner, I decided to raise my personal profile by standing in my local constituency to highlight the problems associated with working in the green economy. I knew that by placing myself in a debating arena with the next MP for my constituency would give me direct access to be able to lobby and hopefully pursuade that person to run with my cause. It was at this time that I started making notes for this book and constructing the various hypotheses on which I would base my arguments.

Crains ran a story on my decision to stand, and within 24 hours I had received a number of calls from journalists wanting a statement from Manchester's first independent candidate to declare an interest in standing at the general election. However, it was a call from home that made the story start to get even more interesting: '*Marcus . . . some guy has just dropped a solicitor's letter off*'.

I can only describe the contents of the letter as an accurate explanation of the situation to date, apart from the fact that I had not at any time questioned B&M's Bromborough operation and their Environment Agency licenses. Recycling is not a legal requirement in the UK and their Bromborough waste plant was irrelevant to the complaint simply because all the evidence was suggesting that the waste collected in Manchester stayed in Manchester, despite what the certificates said. The solicitor set out the fact that their client was entitled to relief from the High Court of Justice in the form of an injunction and I should urgently seek legal advice from a specialist in defamation law. In the letter, B&M also claimed that the visit to Colliers waste tip in Trafford Park that I had observed was a mere contingency plan caused by a breakdown on their primary scheduled route to Bromborough. Most importantly though for some reason the letter included a copy of a long winded, factually incorrect email from B&M's director Terry Milner to Jones Lang Lasalle which said 'I wish to confirm that the recycling certificates for 2 Hardman Square (MEN) are correct' and that they 'would stand up to any audit examinination your landlords, your tenants or yourselves would wish to implement'. He then went onto refer to my claims as being both misleading and somewhat fatuous. The letter must have been drafted by a trainee solicitor straight from college because the first base of any legal correspondence is to never compromise your client when on the offensive. As an auditor, when you have a statement saying that something is correct, it is a starting point to work backwards from.

The rest of the letter was built around the fact (stated in a technical, eloquent and legal manner) that if I didn't shut my mouth, I would probably lose my house, my business and my family security. It also said I should act honourably by sending a letter of apology to B&M retracting my allegations. As expected, B&M was fighting back and it became obvious that I had to stick to the facts without elaborating on the truth.

Chapter 2

The application of basic economics and common sense

'Threats don't work with the person who's got nothing to lose.'

Maduro Ash

Whoever Maduro Ash is or was, the quote above is very relevant here. If you run a business that is finding it hard to compete in its target market place, it is unlikely that it will be awash with cash and assets. STE Waste was, and still is, in that position. Indeed, any threat of legal action will probably tip the firm into the hands of an insolvency practitioner where the creditors' report will simply read: *'Unable to compete in the green economy'*.

As discussed earlier, I had already lost all my personal wealth and a lot more besides, so it is unlikely that anyone would find a treasure chest if they were to pursue me in a UK court of law. I believe the legal technical term for someone like me is a 'man of straw'. The costs of defamation law and of taking someone to the High Court in the UK are astronomical, and then there is the small matter of a trial by jury if the accused refuses to shut his or her mouth. As it stands, a wealthier man would be much more reluctant to defend himself against the threat of defamation law. This situation may change by the end of 2011 in order to protect responsible journalism that is seeking to raise issues in the interests of the general public. This move is currently supported by all three main UK political parties.

When debating any economic issue that is in the public's interest, it stands to reason that there is a need to use economic principles. The green economy is no different and the well-known economic theory of 'Opportunity Cost' played an important part in my complaint to the Environment Agency and Trading Standards. I used this theory to point out why, in business terms, it is ridiculous to think that a waste truck would ever run from Manchester to Bromborough and back again, when there are legal tips in Manchester that can receive the waste. (The environmental impact of the 120 mile round trip is not taken into account here, but it is certainly in keeping with the general argument of the book.)

Opportunity Cost

What Does *Opportunity Cost* Mean?

1. The cost of an alternative that must be forgone in order to pursue a certain action. Put another way, the benefits you could have received by taking an alternative action.
2. The difference in return between a chosen investment and one that is necessarily passed up. Say you invest in a stock and it returns a paltry 2% over the year. In placing your money in the stock, you gave up the opportunity of another investment—say, a risk-free government bond yielding 6%. In this situation, your opportunity costs are 4% (6%—2%).

(Source: Investopedia)

To perform this 120 mile trip in such a large truck would take up four hours of a typical day, allowing for traffic. It would be very expensive in terms of the driver's wages, fuel and other variables. However, it is not the cost of driving to Bromborough which makes this an unlikely primary scheduled route, but rather the time spent not collecting waste and therefore losing income. One of the first rules of business is never to lose time incurring costs when you could be collecting income.

In Manchester, commercial buildings have, on average, five bins lifted each day. My experience in waste logistics tells me that it is feasible to suggest that 25 bins could be lifted each hour in such a densely built up city centre. The going rate at the time was £10 per bin, so simple mathematics gives a potential income of £1,000 for the four hours it would take to get to Bromborough and back. 25 full bins roughly equate to a ton of waste and at the time of my complaint, the gate fees at Colliers and Viridor were around £50 for each ton.

It is easy to see that, in business terms, collecting £1,000 in income and spending £200 at Trafford Park is a much better financial option than incurring running costs with no yield on an expensive four hour round trip to Bromborough. The Opportunity Cost of running trucks from Manchester to Bromborough is therefore extremely high, and I should also point out that this equation is based on a 'per truck per day basis'. You don't need to be a financial genius to work out the kind of figures involved if the company in question has 10 trucks operating in and around Manchester all day, every day.

The MEN recycling certificate referred to the B&M transfer station in Bromborough because until March 2010, this was the only transfer station B&M had that was authorised by the Environment Agency to receive commercial waste. If Manchester's waste was never taken to Bromborough, the certificate is automatically misleading. If numerous buildings in Manchester were receiving identical certificates, it is likely that thousands of companies were affected, many of them high profile. The best evidence that a number of Manchester clients were receiving these certificates is B&M's own newsletter. The Winter 2009/10 edition says that '. . . *clearly with recycling levels for many customers now over 95% and ongoing investment in fleet and facilities the B&M package is compelling*'.

What the certificate for the MEN actually says is that all the compacted waste that is collected is taken all the way to Bromborough to be sorted. Then, the residue is loaded onto another truck and taken to the Orchid processing plant in Huyton, Liverpool to be made into refuse-derived fuel. Given the distance involved, the tip in Huyton also looks an unlikely destination for Manchester's commercial waste, but we only need to look at Orchid's July to September 2009 waste return, reproduced below, to find out the truth about its environmental performance:

Environment Agency — Waste Return

Waste Return

Environmental Protection Act 1990
Pollution Prevention and Control Act 1999

Date of issue:

When completed please E-Mail to:
monitoring.west@environment-agency.gov.uk

* Use this form to tell us the type and quantity of controlled waste you have processed at each facility on your site over the last quarter.

* Please read through the whole form and guidance notes before you start filling anything in.

* Please e-mail the completed form back to us within 28 days of the end of the return period to the address on the left.

1 Return Period

Period name:	Year
Qtr Jul-Sep	2009

2 Operator and site details

Site Operator
Orchid Environmental Limited

PPC Permit or WM Licence no.
50487

Site name
Orchid Environmental Waste Teatment Facility

Site Address

Stretton Way
Huyton
Nr Liverpool
Merseyside

Post Code: L36 6JF

2.2 Waste management facility/operation

A16 – Physical Treatment Facility

2.3 Was a weighbridge used?

	Yes
Percentage weighed	100 %

2.5 If you are not operating a landfill go to section 3

Landfill Sites Only

2.5 Remaining void space covered by licence

2.6 Was the site fully surveyed in the past 12 months?
if no go to question 2.7   Date Surveyed

How was the void space calculated?

2.7 How have you estimated the remaining void space?
For example visually or other method

2.8 Remaining life of site (Years)

Now go to sections 3 and 4 (waste received/removed from site)

5 Declaration

I certify that the information in this return is correct to the best of my knowledge and belief.

Name	J.D. Jump
Position	Logestics Manager
Phone	0151 482 0002
Date	19/10/2009

6 Disclosure and data protection

The information you provide will be used by the Environment Agency to enable it to fulfil its regulatory and waste management planning responsibilities.
For full information on how the data in this form will be used please see the waste return guidance notes.

WASTE RECEIVED ON SITE

Please read the guidance notes before filling in the form

Running total (Amount)	12,573.00

Origin	EWC Waste Code	State	Amount	Units	Additional info					
					final disposal	Used on site	Hazardous	From another facility	Bio'able Municipal	Other Bio'able
North West	200301	Solid	11,735	Tonnes	No	Yes	No	No	Yes	No
North West	191212	Solid	838	Tonnes	No	Yes	No	Yes	Yes	Y

WASTE REMOVED FROM SITE

Please read the guidance notes before filling in the form

Running total (Amount)	10,563.74

Destination	EWC Waste Code	State	Amount	Units	Hazardous	Destination Facility Type
Merseyside	191212	Solid	1,621.00	Tonnes	No	3 - Landfill
Rugby	191210	Solid	3,718.00	Tonnes	No	1 - Incinerator
Manchester	191202	Solid	263.00	Tonnes	No	6 - Recycling
Manchester	191203	Solid	56.00	Tonnes	No	6 - Recycling
Cheshire	191204	Solid	497.74	Tonnes	No	6 - Recycling
Cheshire	191205	Solid	497.00	Tonnes	No	5 - Reprocessing
Lancashire	191212	Solid	3,911.00	Tonnes	No	3 - Landfill

For the period relating to the MEN's recycling certificate, Orchid's waste return shows that the plant only recycled 8% of its waste. 55% was put into landfill and 35% burned. So by simply analysing the information on B&M's own certificate, we can see that their claim of 95% recycling starts to looks misleading if they had indeed taken all their waste to Orchid during this period. Interestingly, the waste is not even made into refuse-derived fuel in Huyton, but is taken to Rugby in Warwickshire by train. Suddenly, the number of miles covered here is looking very environmentally-unsound in terms of carbon footprint and it would also appear that the B&M official audit trail for Manchester's commercial and government waste is not financially viable.

The best way to understand what is going on here is to imagine a cake that has been baked. Beforehand, you know exactly what the ingredients are. They are measured out separately and it would be easy to construct a pie chart showing the cake's composition. However, once the cake has been baked, it is almost impossible to distinguish between the ingredients. It is also impossible to construct an accurate pie chart by just looking at the cake retrospectively. The same principle applies to a lorry load of compacted waste. Unless the lorry is holding a single waste stream such as paper, it would be almost impossible to sort the compacted waste into its various components. To strengthen this argument, I am not sure anyone would be allowed to sort through waste to this extent without breaking the UK's strict health and safety laws, particularly if the load was contaminated with rotten food.

In mid February, my Business Development Manager rang me late one afternoon to say he had just done a waste audit at Hope Hospital in Salford. The hospital had a certificate, issued by B&M, claiming a recycling rate of 94.29%.

A quick search on the internet produced a number of results for 'B&M NHS 95% recycling'. The best example is the one below, taken from an NHS Western Cheshire e-briefing from January 2010 which was repeated in July 2010. The same claims were also made as part of a case study in a document entitled '*Eco Rep's Handbook for Cheshire and Warrington*', which gives NHS staff environmental guidance on everything from waste to energy and water.

'Waste Management

A reminder to all staff concerning our waste management arrangements.

Domestic Waste

In support of the environmental and sustainability work that NHS Western Cheshire are following, our domestic waste is now collected from all of our premises by Bagnall and Morris (B&M) Waste Services.

B&M Waste Services are able to process commercial waste at their Material Recovery Facility. They segregate food, cardboard, paper, glass, rigid plastics and other metals, as well as other specialist items.

The domestic waste from NHS Western Cheshire will be recycled effectively, legally and in a safe environment. Bagnall and Morris guarantee to recycle 95% of domestic waste, and are aiming to achieve 98%.

There is no need for our staff to segregate their domestic waste in any way. *All of the above items can be placed in the black bin bags, with the exception of* **confidential waste** *(see below) and anything that could be considered* **sharp** *(broken cups, bottles, sharp plastic etc.). Anything sharp MUST be wrapped safely before being disposed of in black bin waste to avoid causing injury.'*

So there is no need for NHS staff to segregate the waste in any way because it will be taken back to B&M's plant and sorted into the various streams for recycling. If B&M could make this possible, why do most of us have at least three bins at home to segregate our waste? If there is a way we can 'just chuck it all in the same bin and it will get sorted out somewhere else', why aren't we using it? The only way the NHS could be making these claims is if the B&M sales force was feeding them the information, as surely the NHS would not have made it up in order to tick their own boxes.

If I try to sell my method of real recycling, which I consider to be the most environmentally sound, into NHS Cheshire, there is no chance they would even consider moving to STE Waste and gaining an environmental disadvantage in percentage terms. This would be a backwards step for such a pro-environment government organisation which has documentation it is willing to shout about. It is unlikely they will ever move anyway, because my 11 year old daughter tells me it is mathematically impossible to construct a 120% pie chart. In all honesty, how did these claims get past the North West Collaborative Commercial Agency (NWCCA), which is in charge of NHS procurement in the North West of England?

The implication for the green economy is that both corporate Manchester and the government-run NHS had found a supplier that claimed to offer near environmental perfection. For other companies wanting a slice of the action, this claim basically says: 'Don't bother trying to compete'. To quote the Peel Land and Property press release reproduced earlier in the book, B&M's recycling claims are indeed 'incredible' and 'astounding'. Surely anyone, particularly a competitor, should be allowed to analyse how such a claim is arrived at and either challenge it or look to emulate it? And in the interests of fair trading and the fledgling green economy, a reasonable and environmentally conscious person would surely then expect Trading Standards and the Environment Agency to step in and prosecute in the interests of the UK green economy if the 95% recycling claims were proved not to be true.

Chapter 3

So just who is looking after our environment?

'The perfect bureaucrat everywhere is the man who manages to make no decisions and escape all responsibility.'

Brooks Atkinson

The initial complaint that I made to Trading Standards in January 2010 was farcical to say the least. And it set the tone for the next 15 months. My first phone call was to Manchester Trading Standards, who passed me on to Trafford Trading Standards, who passed me on to Stockport Trading Standards. Stockport eventually decided I should contact The Wirral Trading Standards. The reason for this is that, although the alleged offence happened in Manchester, they argued the problem was in Trafford because the waste was tipped over the council boundary line. Trafford countered that my company was based in Stockport and Stockport then successfully transferred the complaint to The Wirral, home of B&M.

The case was finally passed to The Wirral's Senior Trading Standards Officer, Mr Nick Chesters, to launch an investigation. I knew from the first moment I spoke to him that there would be trouble ahead because he had no idea what I was talking about. Trading Standards in the UK are used to dealing with tangible problems such as fake branded watches or dodgy designer jeans labels. There is usually clear evidence that a crime has taken place and this can easily be proved by the number of people who claim to be victims and are willing to make witness statements. However, my issue was an intangible problem: waste audit trails that did not stack up with recycling certificates that were being used to tick environmental marketing boxes. I appreciate this might be difficult for someone with no experience in the waste industry to understand. Sadly, when you know exactly what you're talking about, it is frustrating when you have no confidence in the organisation that will ultimately decide whether or not to prosecute.

As anyone who works in the waste industry knows, elaborating recycling figures gives you a clear advantage over the genuine companies who give their clients factual information. Yet here was a dustbin man—effectively what I am—saying that very few of Manchester's huge multinational organisations had checked their environmental supply line correctly, and that the corporate and social responsibility statements made by a number of tenants in Manchester's office space were false marketing illusions. Put this way, it is easy to see why Nick Chesters thought I was mad. Why would anyone believe me? And with resources running low and councils suffering cuts left, right and centre, it isn't surprising that my complaint was left on the back burner as a low priority.

It became obvious that Trading Standards did not have the necessary empathy to deal with my case so I decided to make a secondary complaint to the Environment Agency, a government quango based in Warrington. When you run a business based around environmental concerns, I think it is a fair assumption that the Environment Agency will eventually sort out any problems.

The Environment Agency's stated purpose is: '*to protect or enhance the environment, taken as a whole*' so as to promote '*the objective of achieving sustainable development*'. (Taken from the Environment Act 1995, section 4). The Agency's vision is of '*a rich, healthy and diverse environment for present and future generations*'.

(Source: Wikipedia)

The email that I received from John Christey at the Environment Agency was absolutely staggering, but it made his organisation's position quite clear:

> '*Further to your concerns I have considered very carefully the issues raised by your emails.*
>
> *The claims raised by B&M on their sales literature sit outside our regulatory control.*
>
> *The Agency does regulate B&M at its licensed facility at Bromborough and its exemptions at the Trafford Park site. The company is a licensed carrier of waste. The company will provide waste returns for its Transfer Station at Bromborough and keep limited records for the exemptions.*
>
> *The collection and transport of waste is controlled under the Duty of Care and the operation of Colliers Waste Transfer Station and Viridors Waste Transfer Station are regulated under the Environmental Permitting Regulations. I can investigate that these activities are carried out in accordance with their permits. The movements of waste to these sites are likely to be covered by an annual ticket with a simple list of EWC codes and a brief description of the waste. The waste returns of the sites will record the tonnages of the waste in and waste out. All these records I can request and these can be provided to you under the Freedom of Information Act. The Duty of Care Transfer Notes detailing waste from these sites will not identify sources, only EWC codes and brief descriptions on annual tickets.*
>
> *Records of individual weighbridge tickets and the tare weights, the details of operators using the sites, their vehicles, the times they unload waste are the records held by the operators and could be considered by many operators to be commercial and in confidence. These are not required to be reported to the Agency and therefore cannot be requested under the Freedom of Information Act by members of the public.*
>
> *The Agency can request this information under its powers, only when there is evidence that offences have been committed, under the legislation we regulate.*
>
> *In this circumstance to require this information would be exceeding our regulatory authority.*

In relation to your claim the document states the Agency has audited the site. The sentence refers to "the audited waste returns for the Environment Agency . . . ." and could refer to a third party carrying out an audit of the waste returns submitted to the Agency.

In conclusion I am unable at this time to take your complaint any further, however I have spoken with Nick Chesters from Wirral Trading Standards Department and we will be assisting him in his investigation.

Regards, John

John Christey
Environment Officer
Croal Irwell Team
Appleton House
Birchwood Boulevard
Birchwood, Warrington
WA3 7WD'

The Environment Agency is quoted twice on the B&M recycling certificates in question (see chapter 6 NHS March 2009 recycling certificate), so it appears that their name was being used to endorse the certificates' authenticity. Yet Mr Christey confirmed in his email that it was outside the Agency's regulatory control to investigate my complaint. The recycling certificates clearly stated that the waste returns that back up the certificates had been audited—but who was responsible for auditing them?

What the email makes clear is that the Environment Agency was unable to do anything to investigate my claim that tens of thousands of tons of commercial waste from Manchester, passed off as recycled for corporate box-ticking purposes, had actually been put into two tips that did very little commercial recycling. The Environment Agency had access to all the relevant information regarding audit trails and tips. In my opinion, they could have answered my claim within a couple of days simply by asking Viridor and Colliers to provide information on B&M's waste tipping activities at their sites.

This was quickly turning into an impossible situation and I decided to take B&M's solicitor's advice and appoint a quality solicitor of my own to speed up the process. I was advised that if Trading Standards knew there was a solicitor involved, they should take my complaint more seriously. And for STE Waste, it was obvious who that solicitor should be.

Every Thursday morning, STE Waste would take our onsite shredding vehicle into the basement of Halliwells solicitors in Manchester to destroy the contents of 10 large red bins of confidential waste. Normally, waste services are scheduled and we would often arrive at the same time as the vehicle from B&M, which held the general waste management contract with Halliwells. Most weeks, my operatives reported that they had seen all the B&M bins emptied into the same truck, with waste including cardboard, plastics and food from the site's cafeteria all thrown in together. The below extract from Halliwells' corporate statement describes the waste management service they thought they were buying from B&M, and which Halliwells were happy to use as a green marketing tool:

'Waste management

We have been instrumental in getting the building management at each location to enter into contracts with waste disposal companies that have the facility to segregate the office waste off site and recycle everything that is possible to recycle.

This means that all of the office waste collected each day by our cleaners all goes through an offsite separation and segregation process which means very little of our office waste is going to landfill.

This evidence again highlights the fact that recycling is related to economic behaviour when a company is purchasing waste services. Again, choosing a waste management supplier with a high recycling rate enables a company to make green claims for financial reporting and marketing purposes.

Returning to my decision to appoint a lawyer, I was sure that if I could get a meeting with a Halliwells partner, it would be easy to explain what was going on and they would take on my case. I set up a meeting with their specialist in Trading Standards enquiries, and gave my initial view that a few letters to Trading Standards and the Environment Agency would quickly resolve the whole debacle. How wrong could I be! Their response was: '*Stop right there Marcus. We can't take this case any further for you as there is a conflict of interests with B&M being our supplier. We cannot act for you.*'

I was sent a bill for £300 plus VAT for an hour of the solicitor's time (eventually discounted to £270 for goodwill) and that was the end of that. Halliwells did nothing to investigate the matter internally and three months later, the firm went bust, sending shock waves through the UK's legal fraternity. STE Waste was left with £3,000 of unpaid invoices for onsite shredding services, which we had to write off.

I hoped to resolve this situation by simply instructing another solicitor, but I ran into an even bigger problem. It turned out that every solicitor in Manchester with a decent Trading Standards and defamation law department had B&M in their basement collecting their waste. If approached, they would all no doubt claim a conflict of interest and be unable to act on my behalf.

In the end, the only aspect of my case that I took advice on was defamation law, as I had already received several letters from B&M's solicitors threatening me with the worst case scenario. A barrister friend of mine gave me a free hour's audience and in the meeting, I asked him straight questions about the defamation laws being used against me to keep me quiet.

In return, he asked me a few questions:

'Are you telling the truth?'

'*I believe so.*'

Is it an honest opinion based on evidence?

'*Yes.*'

'Can you prove it?'

'*I think so.*'

'Are you working in the interests of the general public?'

'*I believe that I am.*'

'Where is your evidence from?'

'*Mainly government-lodged information that is freely available to the public.*'

As most of us in the UK know, you might seem to be on very firm ground with defamation law, but it is not as simple as that. However, I do have on my side the body of public opinion, particularly of those with a scientific background, who have had enough of people not being able to make responsible criticisms when there is clear evidence to be analysed.

The very idea that, in 2011, someone should be put in a position where they have to risk their whole financial security just to compete in an open market is, quite frankly, draconian.

Chapter 4

The general election 6th May 2010

'The Liberal Democrats are the only party in Britain that can and will put the environment at the heart of government. We'll begin creating our new green economy on day one.'

Nick Clegg, Liberal Party Manifesto 2010

I can honestly say that, when I looked at the general election, I concluded that I had no chance of making an impact on the two issues I was standing on: the green economy and freedom of speech in the public's interest. After all, no one had ever heard of me and everyone else was saying they believed in the green economy too, so there was nothing that made me different enough to justify a vote. And I think it's safe to say that most people in the UK would assume this is a free country where you can analyse information and report what you find without a defamation lawyer throwing his weight around.

I found the green economy to be an interesting subject in this election. All my opponents said they believed in the green economy but when I spoke to them about it, no one seemed to understand it or how it worked. The Green Party is probably the best example. Whilst obviously green-minded, it is my opinion that they lack the business acumen to promote green economics to a mass audience that sees them as a credible alternative. They are certainly a morally-sound pressure group that has done wonders to raise public awareness of environmental concerns, but they lack the key ingredients to do themselves justice on the national stage. Their poor performance at the local voting count suggests I am not the only one with this view. And I don't think it is inappropriate to suggest that the Liberal Democrats also noticed the Green Party's weaknesses and actively courted their supporters to secure votes in key marginal seats.

I firmly believe that the shrewdest political move for the Liberal Democrats would be to create a Green Party coalition at the next general election, to make sure they don't get completely obliterated in the future. The Liberal Democrats don't seem to have had much impact during the first year of the coalition government so they urgently need to do something different for the next election if they are to win back the public's faith. In my opinion, the UK is now ready for a third party to emerge that truly puts the green economy at the heart of its politics instead of just talking about it. And I think both these parties need each other next time around to prevent the UK becoming a two party political system like the USA.

I was contesting the Withington and Didsbury seat, a well-known tight marginal seat that had already turned into the 'Liberal John' and 'Lucy Labour' circus. Both these candidates were bombarding the local electorate with political propaganda that pointed out the other's shortcomings, but didn't say what they would do differently. However, in reality, it was all about how many people wanted to see the end of New Labour. John Leech became the Liberal Democrats MP in 2005, just as New Labour was being rumbled by the professional classes. The talented and gifted Lucy Powell, who was fighting the red corner, was probably five years too late to win this seat. In any case, if your party leader is heard referring to salt of the earth people as 'bigots' and their national policy is to alienate the constituency's strong student population, then it doesn't matter how good you are. Although I would never personally vote for Labour, I found their whole campaign team to be good fun, courteous and civilised.

The biggest let down of this local contest was, without a doubt, the Conservative party. They just didn't seem to have done their homework on the seat I was contesting. History points to the fact that it has strong blue foundations, as between 1931 and 1987 it never changed colour. As an observer, I concluded that at least 10,000 of John Leech's Liberal Democrat votes were tactical Tories waiting for a strong candidate to arrive and put up a decent fight. With no disrespect to Chris Green who fought for the Conservatives, he was never going to make an impact without his national party's support and resources. Unfortunately, the Tories have almost given up in this constituency and seem to think that just turning up is acceptable. Also, in my opinion, the Conservatives' view on environmental issues at this election was unconvincing to say the least. And since then, there has been more interest in the coalition's Energy Minister Chris Huhne's driving licence than in what he has done to promote the green economy and, in particular, environmental autarky (self-sufficiency). It should also be noted that the Environment Secretary, Caroline Spelman, has also so far failed to bring the importance of the green economy to the forefront of British politics.

The other two candidates standing at my local election were Robert Gutfreund-Warmsley of the UK Independence Party (UKIP) and Yasmin Zalzala, who stood independently. I can only describe Robert as an extremely interesting, intelligent and well read man who always made me feel as if I'd learned something when I came away from our conversations—and he may yet prove to be correct about the euro zone. Sadly for Yasmin, she felt betrayed by the Liberal Democrats and her whole campaign seemed to revolve around a claim that the party chose John Leech as a candidate over her for racially motivated reasons.

Out of interest, I asked B&M's solicitor for guidance about what I could and couldn't say in my own campaign. Their reply was exactly what you'd expect from a defamation lawyer. What B&M and their solicitor didn't know was that I had no intention of writing a political manifesto about them, as this would have looked stupid and would also be abusing the political system for commercial reasons. The issue was between STE Waste and B&M, not Marcus Farmer and B&M, and as far as I know a company, despite being a separate legal identity, cannot stand at an election. However, I did open my manifesto with a message about why I was standing, even though it wouldn't have meant anything to anyone at the time. Here is that message:

> *'My reasons for standing*
>
> *'In a time of universal deceit, telling the truth is a revolutionary act.'*
> *George Orwell*

In early 2010, the environmentally sound, forward thinking company of which I am Managing Director found itself in a position where it could no longer compete in an unregulated market with no national policy. What's more, the questions I was putting to the government departments supposedly in place to protect it were falling on deaf ears. I was left with no option but to make a protest for the very survival of my company and others like it.

And what better place to do this than a marginal seat, fighting over 600 votes from the last election, where environmental concerns are a key part of local thinking?

After all, if there is no independent body in place with the powers to protect fair environmental trading and people who have chosen to do the right thing, then any government's dream of a future green economy is exactly that. A dream.

In the past, I always thought this was a free country where people were at liberty to collate evidence and ask simple, science-based questions without fear of retribution. Given my recent experiences, I am no longer sure this is the case.

Due to the situation I am in and the strength of defamation law in our litigious society, I am taking the unique—and bizarre—position in this general election as the only candidate who can't tell his audience what he is protesting against.'

When you go to the town hall and pay your £500 deposit to stand as a candidate, it gets you into the spirit of things. I took a full two months to research and find a different angle on most of the current political arguments. My manifesto is still available to read at www. marcusfarmerindependent.com. It covers a wide range of topics from the legalisation of drugs (argued from Milton Friedman's perspective) to why we should all join the BNP to defeat racism. I dug out a load of philosophy books and used quotes from the most obscure sources, from Ray Honeyford, the Bradford headmaster sold out by the Thatcher government in the mid-eighties (who in my opinion should receive a national apology), to Ibn Warraq, arguably the bravest writer of the last 20 years if relatively unknown outside academic circles. I really enjoyed pulling lots of left-of-field ideas together along with what I considered to be plausible arguments and at the very least I have a document to show my grandchildren how odd my mind was at the age of 40. I also made a number of predictions within the manifesto and, from a personal viewpoint, it will be interesting in the future to see which bits I got right and which I got wrong.

The document was very rushed and is still in 'draft brainstorming on current affairs form', but I gave it my best effort in the short time available. I got several 'Best wishes' and 'Well done' emails from people who said they'd enjoyed reading it. Surprisingly, many of the people who emailed agreed with most of my points but not surprisingly, said they would probably still vote for one of the main parties. In the end I polled just 57 votes (including my own) without any campaigning and I received plenty of banter and backhanded respect with no nastiness. However, the best statistic was that there were only 495 unique visitors to my website before the general election, so when people mock the result I can claim an 11.5% return—and the fact that Jesus Christ started out with only 12 supporters whilst I had 56! More importantly, I had registered my complaint and taken a stand.

As an independent candidate, you are copied into a lot of political stuff that the general public doesn't see. And it became apparent very early on that fighting for a marginal seat in the UK is a very serious business. In fact, it's so serious that everyone is scared stiff of making a mistake so there is a lot of saying nothing and sitting on the fence. It became obvious that 'Lucy Labour' and 'Liberal John' had been briefed to play a safe game and let their respective leaders run the national campaign. I think this is why most people have switched off to politics—it has become boring, predictable and lacking in characters that are willing to express their true views.

Sadly, I did not click with John Leech MP right from the start. When a spoiler comes along (the technical term for an independent candidate in the UK), the political tactics are surely to engage and respect an unknown quantity as they are not really a threat. When I went in to his surgery to introduce myself and wish him luck, I found him very dismissive. In fact, he said I was wasting my time and would lose my deposit. He was certainly correct about the latter and until now, he was also right about the former.

My opinion of him really went downhill when someone put a load of Liberal Democrats posters all over my house during the general election campaign. The security light came on outside my house at about 10pm and I thought nothing of it, but when it stayed on I looked outside and saw a man fitting Mr Leech's description (5'10" with strong features) walking away from my house. I couldn't say for sure it was him, but I reported the incident to the police, who interviewed both of us. It was also reported to the Manchester Evening News (MEN) who came and took photographs but didn't run the story. John Leech made the following statement to the MEN:

> *'I am sorry that Mr Farmer has been dragged into another dirty tricks campaign. This is the second time in days that the emergency services have been called out unnecessarily in smear campaigns against the Liberal Democrats—now the police's time is being wasted by the actions of our opponents. We recently had a visit from the Fire Service after a complaint from a member of the "public". This took fire service staff off our streets too and is unacceptable.*
>
> *This poster has been sent out to thousands of residents in south Manchester. It is a shame that these tactics are diverting attention away from issues during this campaign. Yet again we are discussing smear tactics instead of the issues in the tightest General Election for generations. I have absolutely nothing to gain from this as everyone knows this is a straight fight between us and Labour. I'll let people draw their own conclusions on who is responsible for these actions, intended to smear my name.'*

ENDS

For me, the posters pretty much summed up the election as a petty local battle between the Lib Dems and Labour. In the end, it took me six days to get John Leech MP to remove the posters from my house. In my view, they were his posters so he was responsible for removing them even if he wasn't responsible for putting them up. I asked him to remove them several times, but he only did it when I told him one of my bin lorries with five tons of waste on board was on its way to his office and he had 15 minutes to take the posters down. Ironically, if I had deposited the waste outside Mr Leech's office, I would probably have been prosecuted by the Environment Agency for illegal tipping.

On 6 May 2010, John Leech won the Didsbury and Withington seat in the general election. The voting results were as follows:

John Leech, Liberal Democrats:	20,110
Lucy Powell, Labour:	18,216
Chris Green, Conservative:	5,005
Brian Candeland, Green Party:	798 (1,595 in 2005)
Robert Gutfreund-Walmsley, UKIP:	698
Yazmin Zalzala, Independent:	147
Marcus Farmer, Independent:	57

Liberal Democrats hold

As far as this book and the green economy are concerned, the key statistic here is the Green Party's decline in votes between 2005 and 2010. Along with the student vote on further educational funding, the environment was a hot topic in this seat and most people will agree that John Leech MP used it all the time to gain votes. If the green card is used skilfully to win elections, then surely it is both important and relevant to public interest.

After the general election, John Leech agreed to meet me. Unfortunately, the chemistry was again uneasy as I don't particularly enjoy being spoken to like a naughty seven year old. However, in fairness to him he made enquiries in all the right areas and he was very good at feeding information back. It also became apparent very quickly that when you are making complaints to government departments, copying in an MP on your emails helps ensure that progress is made and you are not ignored. If I hadn't copied in John Leech MP, this situation would probably never have been investigated, and in many ways he became a useful pawn to get things moving. I know he had at least one meeting with B&M's Chief Executive, Mr Peter Cooke, and there was reference in one letter to a meeting with another director, Mr Terry Milner, but I don't know which issues were discussed. I would have loved to have been a fly on the wall though.

To keep the story going in *Crains* business magazine, the editor Steve Bauner printed the below article about my stand at the general election:

> ### 'Gagging for the truth
>
> *Bottom of the poll, but waste company owner's claims should be investigated*
> > *By Steve Brauner, Editor*
>
> *Marcus Farmer, who runs a waste management firm, may have done the least campaigning of any candidate in last Thursday's General Election.*
>
> *He hadn't intended to be so quiet, in public at least, but his manifesto attracted a rather threatening solicitor's letter which had the effect, he says, of gagging him.*
>
> *Farmer, managing director of Cheadle Hulme-based STE Waste Management Ltd, stood as an independent in his home seat of Manchester Withington in the hope of highlighting what he sees as an example of "greenwash". He claims that some of his competitors have led clients*

to believe that the bulk of their waste is being recycled when in reality much of it is going straight to landfill.

He has pointed this out to some of those clients and their reaction has been to turn a blind eye. One reason for this is that they need a certificate saying that 95 per cent of their waste is recycled in order to qualify for the international environmental management standard ISO14001.

Achieving that level of recycling generally requires sorting at source and that is an expensive process. It is Farmer's contention that some companies are not doing any sorting whatsoever and he claims to have proof.

Naturally, his allegations have ruffled a few feathers and prompted one of his rivals to call in a defamation lawyer to fire a shot across his bows.

I make no judgement about the validity of Farmer's claims. But it stands to reason that when demand for a service is created by legislation, there is always the risk that the relevant certificate becomes a more important "product" than the service itself.

Lack of regulatory oversight creates an opportunity for less scrupulous suppliers to supply that certificate more cheaply by cutting corners on carrying out the service. As long as their customers have "plausible deniability", they probably won't enquire too deeply about the suppliers' methods. They may not even notice that the truck which collects their waste paper then picks up waste food from a takeaway and mashes it all up into one lovely mess.

The more you think about it, the more likely it seems that this kind of thing is going on. Farmer may have received only 57 votes, but he shouldn't be dismissed as a monster raving loony.'

In late September 2010, I was approached in a pub by a local man that I vaguely knew. It suddenly clicked that Paul Hardman, who said he was a staunch, diehard Labour party supporter, had been doing a few odd jobs in my garden at the time of the election. He then confessed to putting the posters all over my house in '. . . *a moment of madness*'. I do not know whether Mr Hardman was also responsible for taking fire service staff off the streets or whether he was an official member of the labour party election team.I accepted the sincere apology from this strong-featured man and bought him a pint. We went on to discuss more relevant things, such as how many points Manchester United would have over Manchester City at the end of the football season and whether Liverpool FC would offer a genuine title challenge.

Chapter 5

Trading Standards and the Environment Agency meet

'Complex, statistically improbable things are by their very nature more difficult to explain than simple, statistically probable things.'

Richard Dawkins

After the general election, it was obvious my complaint was still on Nick Chester's desk at Wirral Trading Standards and he had done nothing about it. Just as I was starting to think the complaint would never be investigated, I received an unexpected email from John Christey at the Environment Agency:

'Further to your email

The Agency has been acting in accordance with Cabinet Office, General Election Guidance 2010 which applied to you as a prospective parliamentary candidate. As the Government has now been elected the purdah period is now lifted and the Agency is now able to respond more comprehensively to your concerns.

An appointment to meet with Gordon Whitaker who is Area Environment Manager for Greater Manchester has been arranged for 10.30 am on May 28th. Please confirm your intention to attend.

Regards, John'

So a member of the general public makes a complaint to the public sector law enforcement bodies, but they can't investigate it because the complainant is standing as a candidate at the general election. I find this staggering, especially as it gave B&M plenty of time to start covering their tracks. For example, one thing my drivers noticed was the number of B&M bins that now had various recycling labels on them. In fairness to Mr Christey, he obviously realised there was a serious problem and he was actually instrumental in drawing all the Trading Standards people together.

The meeting with the Environment Agency took place in Warrington. I sat down with John Christey and his line manager, Gordon Whittaker, and we discussed the issue in detail for over an hour. Both men were unimpressed that the Environment Agency's name appeared on the certificates in question and went on to explain their organisation's role in depth. The Environment Agency's powers stopped at making sure that waste was transferred correctly from producer (tenant) to carrier (waste company) and then in turn to a legal tip. No one was suggesting that B&M were throwing all their collected waste in a farmer's field and they were certainly using bona fide tips authorised by the Environment Agency to receive waste. But what about the environmental claims they were making on their certificates? Until this point I had believed that everything environmental came under the Environment Agency's remit—but as it turned out, I was wrong.

Mr Christey went on to say that the biggest problem in these cases was that companies under question always turned up with the best lawyers, making prosecution very complicated. I already knew the lengths some companies will go to make sure they are not taken to court, but I still thought this was an odd thing to say. John Christey later confirmed the outcome of our meeting by email:

> *'Hi Marcus*
>
> *Thank you for attending the meeting today with myself and Gordon Whitaker, Environment Manager for Greater Manchester.*
>
> *I was pleased that you were happy with our approach and concurred that the primary legislator in this case is the Trading Standards department situated across the boroughs. As stated in the meeting, we will continue to support the Trading Standards Officers from Wirral, Trafford and Manchester in their ongoing investigation of your complaint and offer our knowledge and expertise whenever required.*
>
> *Can we reiterate that we understand your concerns and difficulties and will do all that we can to assist in the resolution of the problem.*
>
> *Regards, John'*

This email copied in all the Trading Standards people who were involved, ensuring there was an audit trail I could refer to. I was not entirely in agreement that I was happy with the Environment Agency approach but I was happy that an audit trail of responsibility to investigate the claim was starting to build. The key part of the email is the last sentence which confirms that the Environment Agency clearly understood exactly what I was talking about, and I got the impression that I wasn't the first person who had made this kind of complaint. As far as I was concerned the issue that had been discussed with Mr Christey and Mr Whitaker was as clear as daylight but for some reason grey clouds started to appear over the coming months.

Next, the various Trading Standards services in Trafford, Manchester and Wirral met with the Environment Agency in Warrington. I would have loved to have been a fly on the wall whilst they decided who was going to investigate my complaint as I suspected no one wanted it on their desk due to lack of resources. In the end, the case was assigned to Manchester Trading Standards.

So, Mr Christey had successfully transferred full responsibility for investigating my case to Trading Standards—even though the claims I was making specifically referred to aspects of the environment covered by the Environment Agency. Once again, a general theme of passing the buck between public sector departments was starting to develop.

Manchester Trading Standards' web page mission statement states that:

> '*Our aim is:*
> **To promote and encourage a fair and safe environment for both consumers and businesses in Manchester.*'

I immediately contacted them to point out that this could turn into a massive case with implications for a number of organisations in the city who were making corporate and social responsibility claims about waste management. I also made it clear that the case was urgent because STE Waste was having problems with its ability to compete in the marketplace. I received the following reply from Mr Peter Duffin who had been assigned the case:

> '*Marcus*
>
> *I understand both your complaint and your sense of urgency. It could indeed be a massive case and that has implications for Trading Standards Services with limited resources. There is also the complication for Trading Standards of the different jurisdictions. The purpose of the meeting on Thursday is to try to sort these things out.*
>
> *Pete Duffin*
> *Trading Standards Specialist*
> *Trading Standards Service*
> *Neighbourhood Services*
> *1 Hammerstone Road Manchester M18 8EQ*'

When I eventually met with Mr Duffin and his line manager Mr Neil Geddes in June 2010, I got the impression that they felt the Environment Agency had dumped this issue on them. Also, I immediately picked up on a negative political vibe around the two organisations which was never going to help STE Waste. They confessed that Trading Standards lacked the necessary expertise or resources to do my complaint justice, and they also argued that the Environment Agency had its own Trading Standards department which should have been given the case. Despite this negativity, at this stage I was just happy that somebody was taking my complaint seriously.

However, it soon became obvious that someone else, or another organisation, had been asked to explain my complaint to Manchester Trading Standards. Both Pete and Neil had an array of waste returns on their desk during the meeting. They confirmed that, according to B&M's own information lodged with the Environment Agency, the waste collected in Manchester did not go to Bromborough but the certificates in question and testimonials on their website clearly referred to the Bromborough site. It was agreed that the commercial waste collected by B&M in Manchester had effectively disappeared and could not be accounted for due to the fact that the recycling certificates could not be reconciled with B&M's waste returns. For some reason, they didn't think the tipping totals for Colliers and Viridor were relevant, something I still don't understand. Mr Christey had already confirmed by email that Manchester Trading Standards had the tonnage figures for waste tipped by B&M at both Viridor and Colliers, and this was ultimately the key evidence for my case. I received two emails from Manchester Trading Standards that summed up their position:

'Marcus

I have requested a meeting with our legal team to assess what level of evidence would satisfy them. I have discussed this at length with my Principal Officer, Neil Geddes, and we are of the opinion that what you are alleging is a large-scale fraud and that is why I have tried to get GMP Economic Crime Unit to take this on, so far without success. We feel that we do not have the resources for this case and that is why we are seeking input from our legal team.

Pete Duffin
Trading Standards Specialist
Trading Standards Service
Neighbourhood Services
1 Hammerstone Road Manchester M18 8EQ'

I asked a few more questions and Neil Geddes finally confirmed their angle of investigation, which I considered to be very narrow and limited but in keeping with an organisation that lacked resources. This is the second email I received:

'Good afternoon Mr Farmer,

I thought we had made our position clear on Tuesday when you came to give Peter Duffin your statement.

The Trading Standards Service is currently looking into your complaint under:

"The Business Protection from Misleading Marketing Regulations 2008 SI No 1276."

Regulation 3 prohibits advertising which misleads traders. The Regulations state at:

"Regulation 3(1)—Advertising which is misleading is prohibited."

"Regulation 3(2)—Advertising is misleading which—

(a) in any way, including its presentation, deceives or is likely to deceive the traders to whom it is addressed or whom it is reaches; and by reason of its deceptive nature, is likely to affect their economic behaviour; or

(b) for those reasons, injures or is likely to injure a competitor."

Regulation 3(3) determines whether advertising is misleading.

It has been explained to you by Mr Duffin that we believe we can show the recycling reports you mention, issued by Bagnall & Morris, are misleading.

Our investigation is concentrating on the Environment Agency Returns by Bagnall & Morris from their Bromsborough depot (Transfer Station). The claims in their recycling reports relate specifically to that depot. Indeed the "testimonials" on the Bagnall & Morris website refer to that depot. Therefore there is no need for us to consider what levels of waste they tip at other sites.

The Environment Agency Returns show where the waste is from, where it goes, method of disposal (landfill, re-processing, recycling etc.) and as I advised you on Tuesday you can request these Returns from John Christey at the Environment Agency, whom you have previously met in respect of this matter, under Freedom of Information Act 2000. I am aware you previously requested, and received, similar Environment Agency Returns from other sites under FOI legislation from Mr. Christey.

We accept that you are an injured party as you have now given us details of contracts your business has lost as a result of these recycling reports from Bagnall & Morris.

We know we need to speak to various Building Managers in Central Manchester to establish whether we can obtain sufficient evidence to prove the recycling reports deceived traders and affected their economic behaviour.

Our next step is to agree with Legal Services the level of evidence we need to obtain to satisfy the requirements to institute legal proceedings under the said legislation.

As you know we meet next week with "legal" to discuss this matter.

You are also aware that Mr. Duffin has contacted the Greater Manchester Police Economic Crime Section to discuss this complaint. They have indicated to us that they would be unlikely to take forward this complaint as an investigation.

Therefore to answer your question I do not think at this time there is any chance of Trading Standards being able to pass this to the police. However there is no reason why you do not report the matter yourself.

In conclusion, we will update you on matters as and when we feel it appropriate, you will be advised when our investigation is complete and its outcome.

In the mean time I would be obliged if only matters directly related to our line of enquiry are forwarded to us.

Regards,

Neil Geddes
Temporary Principal Trading Standards Specialist
Manchester City Council'

The most noticeable fact here is that Neil Geddes confirms that whilst he and Peter Duffin think the certificates are misleading, they need to link them to economic behaviour to prove an offence has taken place. My impression was that even though they were certain an offence had indeed been committed, my witness statement was worthless. In other words, it doesn't matter whether the recycling certificates for the whole of corporate Manchester are false or if the waste is dumped in a waste tip that doesn't recycle, because unless a facilities management company comes forward and say in a witness statement that B&M has misled them about their recycling figures, the case would fall apart.

Looking at it cynically, you could say this was always unlikely to happen as no middle man (i.e. a facilities management company) would want the controversy of getting their environmental waste supply line wrong. That could open the floodgates to law suits from tenants who have relied on the recycling reports to make their environmental marketing statements and from landlords who have employed them to get the best services for their clients. The same cynic would therefore fully understand the commercial reasons why such a middle man would choose to remain quiet when asked for a witness statement. The facilities management companies in Manchester are a small parish of very powerful people who control huge procurement budgets and who regularly liaise and exchange ideas with each other. They all make statements about sustainability and environment concern on their websites as part of the marketing mix in order to entice landlords and tenants, so it makes sense that they would always employ the supplier who provides the best environmental performance for any product or service linked to the environment so long as the price is competitive.

Once the Environment Agency had moved my complaint along, the reality was that it was always going to be a losing battle. I was resigned to the fact that, due to lack of resources and expertise, this was never going to be easy. But when I came away from the meeting, I was still confident it wouldn't take them long to prove my claims were right. The downside here is that you only have to do a quick Internet search and look at what Trading Standards do and what their powers are to see they were totally out of their depth and they should not have been in charge of the case. To make matters worse, Manchester City Council was having serious budget issues and the cuts were already starting to run deep.

When you combine the green 'Liberal Left' ethos promoted by Manchester City Council with the politics of the expensive former Labour administration, found to be in disarray since May 2010, it is obvious that a case like this would raise serious questions around the activities of the environment officers employed by the Council to promote and protect Manchester's green concerns. This was a time to defend public sector jobs, not one to show them up as worthless. And it wasn't difficult to dismiss the lone bin man shouting about morality in the green economy—all they had to do was find a reason not to prosecute. So in hindsight, the odds were severely stacked against any prosecution, especially when you consider the lack of specific green law and clear government policy. Arguably then, the path of least resistance was the most attractive here to follow for an organisation lacking resources and expertise in a specific area.

Because I lacked faith in the Trading Standards investigation, I started to feed Peter and Neil all sorts of relevant information, including the fact that B&M had started tipping hundreds of tonnes of waste a month at Davidson's waste station which I knew had no recycling facilities.

The interesting part of this is that Davidson's went into liquidation soon afterwards, leaving all B&M's waste in the open air. It is still there at the time of writing—12 months after I received the below email—and grass is now starting to grow on the 5,000 tonne plus pile.

Peter Duffin's email reply confirms this was not their line of enquiry, but it also made clear that he was the only one working on it. All he had to do was request vehicle tracking devices from B&M and match the certificates to the waste audit trail and he would have had his evidence. But, as his email shows, they weren't interested in this approach:

> 'Marcus
>
> No, I don't want to know. We have explained several times that we do not have the resources to try to trace waste from particular buildings to particular sites and then try to get waste reports from occupants of those buildings. We are relying on B&M's waste returns to the EA contradicting claims made for their Bromborough site along with those returns showing that no waste was received from Manchester. Please do not send me anymore anecdotal evidence. In any case I am on leave for the next two weeks.
>
> Pete Duffin
> Trading Standards Specialist
> Trading Standards Service
> Manchester'

At this point, it is important to note Mr Duffin's comment that '*We are relying on B&M's waste returns to the EA contradicting claims made for their Bromborough site along with those returns showing that no waste was received from Manchester.*' In my desparation for information and protection I forgot to ask Mr Duffin whether or not he had a nice time.

On a positive note, I knew I had a quality journalist that completely understood my predicament and was willing to report on any developments. And the fact that a waste company was being investigated by Manchester Trading standards for environmental fraud did hit the front page of *Crains* business magazine. But sadly, this was to be their last edition.

> 'Hi,
>
> You may have read the breaking news on our own website that Crain's Manchester Business is sadly closing down.
>
> We are all very proud of our achievements in the past few years having built a trusted brand from scratch. (From laptops at Manchester Business Park in Summer 2007!!!)
>
> Thank you for all your support and reading Crain's in the past few years.'

What do you mean you've gone bust?

Chapter 6

The NHS

'Price is what you pay, value is what you get.'

Warren Buffet

I think it's safe to say that any company supplying products and services to the government would class this as the jewel in the crown of their client portfolio for two reasons. Firstly, the relationship is very low risk, especially if the company is under contract, as they are guaranteed to get paid and secondly, having the kudos of working for the government makes selling to other organisations much easier as it is almost a rubber stamp of approval. A glowing testimonial from the NHS is therefore worth its weight in gold.

Having said that, any government supplier is also open to public scrutiny so they need to make sure they supply what they say they're supplying. The NHS, like most taxpayer-funded organisations, has clear counter-fraud and whistleblower policies in place and it is relatively easy for a member of the general public to analyse and question any of their activities under the Freedom of Information Act and then report the findings without fear of retribution. At least, that is the theory.

NHS Manchester's counter-fraud policy gives a clear definition of fraud:

'The intentional distortion of financial statements or other records by persons internal or external to the organisation which is carried out to conceal the misappropriation of assets or otherwise for gain.'

The policy also sets out the three fundamental public service values which underpin the NHS and all public sector work:

'Accountability: Everything done by those who work in the organisation must be able to stand the tests of Parliamentary scrutiny, public judgements on propriety and professional codes of conduct.

Probity: Absolute honesty and integrity should be exercised in dealing with NHS patients, assets, staff, suppliers and customers.

Openness: The organisation's activities should be significantly public and transparent to promote confidence between the organisation and its patients, staff and the public.'

Having already looked at Hope Hospital, it was time to turn my attention to NHS Manchester for two reasons. Firstly, it was my local NHS trust and as a taxpayer, I have a right to analyse how it spends its money. And secondly because their facilities manager appeared twice in the testimonials section on B&M's website, clearly endorsing their services to the general public. A testimonials page on a commercial website is there for one purpose: so other organisations can refer to it for references. One of the two letters on the website, both of which are free for anyone to access under the Freedom of Information Act, read as follows:

Manchester Community Health

Ms W. Mitchell
Bagnall & Morris
Taylor Road
Trafford Park
Urmston
Manchester
M41 7JQ

NHS Manchester
Mauldeth House
Mauldeth Road West
Chorlton
Manchester
M21 7RL
Tel: 0161 958 4003
Fax: 0161 958 4040
Email: peter.kevan@manchester.nhs.uk

19th May 2009

Dear Wendy,
Just a quick note to thank you and your team on the service provided by B&M.

Bagnall & Morris ensured that NHS Manchester had a smooth changeover and an exceptional service from day one. Any operational issues have been few and minor and dealt with in a fast professional manor. NHS Manchester can now prove our recycling figures thanks to the quarterly environmental reports. B&M are a vast improvement from our previous general waste contractor.

Yours sincerely

Peter Kevan
Contract Manager

Mr Kevan clearly thought he could prove the NHS recycling figures so I wrote to him to try and get some more information. He was very genuine and courteous, and gave me his honest opinions and a useful insight into the NHS's waste management procurement strategy. The emails reproduced below show that the NHS North West's Procurement Hub had approved B&M as an authorised supplier, so it makes sense that Mr Kevan would think his organisation had the best available waste strategy—particularly as there was a detailed recycling certificate to back up the claims. The point that must be made here is that the NHS has plausible deniability just like every other organisation that received a similar certificate and it is human nature to assume the information we receive is correct. A comparison can be made with sophisticated ponzi schemes where everyone assumes everything is above board until someone points out that it isn't. And more often than not, the first reaction is denial.

Here is the email trail between myself and Mr Kevan after I sent him a letter introducing myself.

'Dear Mr Farmer,

Thank you for your recent letter and brochure.

NHS Manchester PCT is currently contracted for our general waste and re-cycling and shredding.

We are currently very happy with our current waste contractors and the recycling figures achieved.

We are not due to tender these services for 4 years approximately.

Kind Regards

Peter Kevan
Facilities Manager'

'Hi Peter

Thanks for your email.

We employ a sort at source method of waste disposal which our research suggests you currently DO NOT use. Paper in particular is a commodity that should all be shredded at your buildings and then taken as clean to a recycling station.

In order to trade waste commodities it is important that you sort all materials at source in order to maximise their value on the open international markets. Your current method leads to contamination which means that it is likely to be landfilled as it cannot be traded.

At present, as waste consultants as well as waste carriers, we simply do not understand how you are making the most of recycling opportunities given the method that you use (i.e. everything in the same bin mixed with other organisations' waste to be sorted elsewhere).

We also do not understand why the government is using such a method in the NHS when we all have sort at source methods at our domestic properties which are proven to maximise recycling levels

My argument against this method is that the NHS is actually losing an opportunity to save money by raising the value of its waste commodities to be traded.

SOW (sorted office waste paper) Paper in particular is currently trading at around £75 delivered to a baling plant.

You can actually track all the prices yourself at www.Letsrecycle.com.

Just out of interest, what do you actually recycle at NHS Manchester because you should have an accurate recycling report from your current contractor?

Marcus Farmer'

'Hi Marcus,

Thanks for your response.

We do receive regular reports giving the recycled amounts of different waste streams. They also provide information on the amount of waste that is turned in to alternative fuel at the Defra approved site.

My view is that why segregate at all when we can turn the waste in to alternative fuels and reduce the number of trucks on the road and also the number of recycling bins in each office / department / building especially when space is in such short supply.

As you are aware most waste sorted on site is usually contaminated which results in the waste going to landfill anyway. This is my experience from this and other facilities posts that I have held over the years, but I don't think we will agree on this point after reading your email below.

We also carry out duty of care audits and follow all of our contractors for both clinical and general waste and conduct site visits both announced and unannounced.

Not sure who supplies you with your research but I don't think it is accurate. Any confidential waste is treated separately with a different contractor and shredded on site.

Also as an organisation and going through the tender process NHS Manchester selected the best contractor for us and the most cost effective. Since NHS Manchester appointed our current supplier they have been approved by the North West Procurement hub. As previously stated we have a contract for the next 4 years so we have no intention of changing supplier.

Thank you for your thoughts and ideas.

Kind Regards

Peter Kevan
Facilities Manager'

'Hi Peter

I know that you are a facilities manager but I am confused at what you say and it seems to contradict best environmental practice.

The environment agency policy is strictly reduce, reuse, recycle but you seem to be advocating that reusing is also burning.

Then you say that you receive regular recycling reports giving the amounts of different waste streams, which seems to indicate that it goes to another site for post sorting before it goes to the approved Defra site.

How does this get sorted if it is all mixed in together (or contaminated)? I can only conclude that 100% must get turned into energy as it would go against British Standards health and safety for it to be manually sorted. This is why we all pre sort in our homes because waste is not possible to recycle efficiently when it is mixed in together.

Running a waste management business I know exactly what the load of compacted mixed waste tipped looks like and I would conclude that it is almost impossible to sort. I would be very interested to see how this is done.

At STE waste we have tracking devices which show exactly what type of waste is put in each truck and where it goes adding to the audit trail. You should also be able to request these tracking reports and information from any supplier which adds to your audit trail.

As you probably know, duty of care audits can actually be verified by waste returns presented to the environment agency for various sites which shows origin of waste and how it is processed, percentages etc. Coming from a scientific academic background my research is always based on evidence and it is actually a fact that transfer stations that manage specific waste streams (glass, plastic, paper, cardboard etc) on the whole perform so much better than the method that you use currently use so perhaps I should liaise with the NWCCA to ask why they selected the 'sort off site method'.

I guess at this stage we disagree on what is environmental and what is not.

Thanks for returning my emails and please don't take my asking questions as trying to cause trouble. All I want is for you to choose the best methods available even if you do not use the services of STE Waste.'

'Hi Marcus,

I do not have time to respond to all of your queries. It is enough to say that we are complying with all rules and regulations and that it is not 100% that is turned to energy. Although turning waste that cannot be recycled in to alternative fuels is much better than sending it to landfill, obviously Defra agree with this.

We do have the producer returns etc but in addition conduct duty of care audits as required.

We have a legitimate and approved supplier with the correct documentation that states the amounts of recycled specific waste streams and we believe that we are using the best method for NHS Manchester and a number of other trusts do as discussed at best value group meetings.

I think that is enough on this subject.

Kind Regards

Peter Kevan'

So NHS Western Cheshire, Hope Hospital and NHS Manchester PCT (all of which fall under the remit of the NHS North West Procurement Hub) all had B&M on their premises using the same method of 'chuck it all in the same bin and we'll sort it out somewhere else'. This was thought to be best value, especially given the recycling claims B&M were making.

Regarding NHS Manchester PCT's waste management policy written by David McGarrigan, Mr Kevan's line manager, there is a contradiction here with what it clearly says in section 2:

'A large quantity of waste output is generated by the trust. It is necessary to segregate and grade the waste before it is disposed of or recycled.'

I decided to do a lot more digging under the Freedom of Information Act and managed to extract a full audit of B&M undertaken by Mr Kevan on 4 January 2010, just before I lodged my complaint with Trading Standards. This has been reproduced below:

Manchester Community Health
Facilities Directorate
Waste Audit – Bulk Waste Collection

Audit Details

Location:		Auditor: PETER KEVAN
Date: 4 01 10		Time:
Service: GENERAL WASTE		Contractor: BAGNALL + MORRIS

Vehicle Details

Plates: NOT APPLICABLE	Condition: GOOD

Driver Details

ADR Licence:	N/A	Photo ID:	
Tremcard :	N/A.	Wheel chock:	
Security Training:		Equipment List on Vehicle:	
Torch (working):		Hi Viz Jacket:	
Warning Signs (x2);		Fire Extinguishers – Dry Power 2Kg & 6Kg – Sealed, Indate for service?	
PPE as per Tremcard:	N/A.	Consignment Note:	N/A.

Any comments on above

	GENERAL WAST AUDIT.

Start Collection Point:

Location: BROMLEY GREEN	Time: 06-45 - VEHICLE ARRIVED 07-16
Details Did the vehicle demonstrate sufficient safety precautions on arrival and parking at site – reversing procedure?	**Response** YES
Was the vehicle locked when left unattended?	DRIVER REMAINED IN CAB
Are the carts in locked areas?	VARIES FROM SITE TO SITE
Are the locked areas clean?	YES
Are the cart lids locked? Are the carts overfilled?	
Are the carts damaged in any way?	No
Did the driver demonstrate appropriate safety precautions when loading/unloading the vehicle?	YES.
Did the driver secure the waste container in the vehicle?	TIPPED IN VEHICLE, CONTAINER RETURNED TO COMPOUND/AREA.
Did any spillage occur during collection?	No
Was the site/storage compound left clean and secure?	YES

Transportation Rout

Collection Point: 1	
Location: BROWNLEY GREEN	**Time:** 07-16
Observations: VEHICLE EMPTIES 2 BINS.	

Collection Point: 2	
Location: NORTHENDEN	**Time:** 07-35
Observations: BINS EMPTIED	

Collection Point: 3	
Location: NORTHEN MOOR	**Time:** 07-43
Observations: OK	

Collection Point: 4	
Location: WITHINGTON CLINIC ''	**Time:** 08-02
Observations: OK	

Collection Point: 5	
Location: CHORLTON	**Time:** 08-17
Observations: OK.	

Please continue on additional sheets for further collection points

Driver Performance

Details	Yes/No

Did the driver demonstrate compliance with the following transport regulation whilst en-rout.
   1. Speed
   2. Traffic priority
   3. Traffic Lights
   4. Public crossings
   5. Parking regulations
	
	1. YES
	2. YES
	3. YES
	4. NOT OBSERVED
	5. YES

Waste Disposable Site

Disposable Site: COLLIERS	
Date: 4/01/10	Time:
Comments/Further information: ACCESS NOT REQUIRED UNDER THIS DUTY OF CARE AUDIT.	

PCT Representative:

P. K—
PETER KEVAN

Date:
4/01/10

The audit shows that Mr Kevan could not prove his recycling figures and if he'd put his head around the gate of Colliers tip, he would have seen that none of his waste was recycled at all. As always, 100% of the waste that entered this site found its way to landfill. As someone who runs a waste company, to me this duty of care audit trail looks more like a driving test for a commercial HGV driver than anything to do with following waste to its destination. Given the short distances and times between the collections and the fact that they don't appear to have had any available time to collect waste from any other organisations, this waste audit looks like it has been set up. And watching a waste collector collecting waste when they know they are being watched doesn't strike me as a good use of public money, especially when there is no interest in what actually happens to the waste.

The recycling certificates given to NHS Manchester PCT, sourced under the Freedom of Information Act and reproduced below, tell their own story. Put side by side, they are the best evidence in this case. The issue date for the 2009 certificate corresponds almost exactly with the date of Peter Kevan's testimonial letter on B&M's website, shown earlier in this chapter. This certificate is signed off by Paul Newton, B&M's Senior National Accounts Manager for NHS clients. B&M's Winter 2009/10 newsletter claims their deal with NHS North West '. . . *was secured through a combination of B&M's high quality service and outstanding environmental performance.*' In the same newsletter, Paul Newton says: '*B&M has proved itself in this difficult arena and shown that it has the flexibility and professionalism to succeed*'. He then adds that: '*It is particularly satisfying to assist these organisations not only to deal with their waste efficiently and cost effectively, but also to do so in an environmentally responsible way*'. It would therefore appear that Mr Newton confirms B&M's opinion that recycling and environmental performance is linked to economic behaviour in the NHS.

Manchester PCT's recycling certificates for 2009 and 2010:

B&M Waste Services

Environmental Recycling Report

General Recycling Performance

For the quarter *January 2009* to *March 2009* the audited 'Waste Returns' for the Environment agency show Bagnall & Morris Transfer station and recycling centre achieved **84.92%** efficiency. This means that for every 1000 tonnes of general waste processed via our transfer station and recycling centre, **849.2 tonnes** of commercially viable recyclable materials were recovered from the waste and diverted from landfill and put back into the market place. The breakdown of the materials recycled from received waste was as follows:

Paper & Cardboard	53.77%
Glass	12.98%
Plastics	12.41%
Metals	3.20%
Wood	2.56%

Below is the prospective recycling performance for your company (extrapolated from the Bagnall & Morris General Recycling Performance). This information may be useful to support your company's environmental policy or ISO 14001 accreditation.

Manchester PCT

Weekly weight: 3.74 tonnes / week

Quarterly Weight: 48.61 tonnes

Weight of recycled: 41.28 tonnes

Breakdown of recycled materials

Paper & Cardboard:	26.14 tonnes
Glass:	6.31 tonnes
Plastics:	6.03 tonnes
Metals:	1.56 tonnes
Wood:	1.24 tonnes

Material to Landfill

Landfill:	7.33 tonnes

The above figures are based on an industry accepted figure of 55kg of waste per cubic metre. The quantities stated are verified by the Environment Agency as being a true and accurate representation and although individual company figures are based only on general figures, they provide accurately estimated indicative evidence of recycling performance from their collections.

Signature: Paul Newton

Date: 15/05/2009

B&M Waste Services
Iris House, Dock Road South, Bromborough, Wirral, CH62 4SQ
Telephone: 0151 346 2900 **Fax:** 0151 346 1309
Email: info@bagnallandmorris.com **Website:** www.bagnallandmorris.com

Registered in England 3473370 VAT No: 733 1774 37

B & M Waste Services Environmental Report

Manchester PCT

This report shows your total recycling/recovery figure to be: **45.9%**

The waste is processed as follows:

Site Address:
All Sites

Account Number:
Various

Date Period:
01/01/2010 to 31/03/2010

Below is the Environment Report for the waste collected from your site for the above period. This information is calculated from the recycling/recovery performance figures provided by the relevant recovery centre/treatment facility that received your waste during this period. This report is calculated from the vehicle route(s) that your site was on and is pro rata based on the size, type, bulk density, quantity of bin(s) on the site. See the detailed report for more information.

Site Segregated Glass (kg)	Site Segregated Recyclables (kg)	Non-Segregated Recyclate (kg)	Refuse Derived Fuel Process (kg)	Residual Waste (kg)	Total Collection Weight (kg)	Total Percentage Recycled/ Recovered
0	832	14319	10819	30330	56100	45.9%

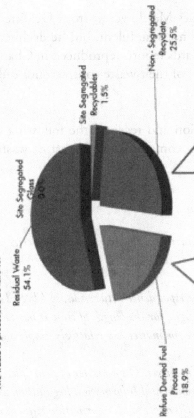

Residual Waste 54.1%

Site Segregated Glass 0%

Site Segregated Recyclables 1.5%

Non - Segregated Recyclate 25.5%

Refuse Derived Fuel Process 18.9%

Non-Segregated Recyclate Breakdown

Plastic 8%
Wood 65%
Metal 8%
Glass 1%
Fertiliser 18%

This pie chart represents the typical composition of the recovered materials processed through a Materials Recovery Facility.

Refuse Derived Fuel (RDF) Process Breakdown

Metals 2%
Glass 6%
Plastics 5%
Moisture 20%
Fuel 67%

This pie chart represents the typical composition of the RDF process. Recyclable materials are recovered prior to fuel preparation.

Carbon Footprint Limited Endorsement

Carbon Footprint Limited have endorsed the service provided by *B & M Waste and agents*, which has reduced your indirect carbon emissions through landfill diversion. These carbon savings equate to:

Carbon Saved (kg)	Equivalent No. of Trees	Equivalent Car Miles*
19,298	26	6,205

*Car miles based on VW Passat 2.0 litre diesel

B & M Waste Services, Iris House, Dock Road South, Bromborough, Wirral, CH62 4SQ
Telephone: 0151 346 2900   **Fax:** 0151 346 1309   **Email:** info@bagnallandmorris.com
Registered in England 3433350   VAT no. 793 1774 37

By now, B&M knew they were being investigated by Trading Standards and the Environment Agency so you would expect the 2010 certificate to be more realistic. Putting the certificates side by side, 2009's incredible 85% recycling rate, signed off by Paul Newton, has dropped to 46% in just 12 months. And this includes 19% accounted for by the refuse-derived fuel process, which wasn't included in the 2009 figure. Only 27% of NHS Manchester PCT's waste was actually recycled in 2010, of which just 1.5% was sorted on site.

The salient point here is that between the two certificate dates, NHS Manchester PCT confirmed by letter to John Leech MP that it didn't change its method of waste disposal, so why are the two recycling certificates so different in percentage terms for each waste category? Both certificates are stamped with ISO 14001 approval authorised by NQA who are affiliated with the chartered institute of waste management. The recycling statistics are there for analysing performance, so I would be keen to read any report which explains why the recycling performance has almost halved and why burning waste is seen as an environmentally friendly option for the NHS in my local constituency. Again, the 2009 certificate seems to indicate that the waste goes all the way to Bromborough to be recycled. It makes reference to B&M's 'Transfer station and recycling centre' and, at the time, Bromborough was B&M's only waste transfer station authorised to process commercial waste.

The less said about the carbon footprint endorsement the better because there are so many varibles that will not have been included in arriving at this figure, and I'll discuss the UK's fixation with saving trees in detail in the final chapter.

I asked the local counter fraud specialist, James Meadowcroft from Deloitte & Touche, for an email to explain why the 2009 certificate was not fraudulent, but he declined my request. The reason becomes apparent in the Trading Standards report, reproduced in Chapter 8, which states that the NHS did not include recycling as part of their waste contract, nor did they take control of where the waste was taken.

I asked NHS Manchester for more information and received the following email from a very helpful Mr Turner on 28 February 2011. My comments on the list of waste transfer stations provided by Mr Turner are shown in brackets.

> *'Dear Mr Farmer*
>
> *I am emailing following your request for an internal review of your queries about waste management.*
>
> *There has been a considerable amount of correspondence between us, so I hope I will be able to settle the matter with my response. I apologise for the length of time it has taken for your review to be dealt with, especially as I believe the matter is a relatively simple one.*
>
> *The original response that you received was incorrect. On a matter of principle, your request should have been dealt with under the Environmental Information Regulations 2004, rather than the Freedom of Information Act. The EIRs apply to all information requests about waste and recycling.*

Information requests to NHS Manchester were being dealt with by a temporary member of staff when your request was received, and we did not get sufficient clarity about what you were asking for. I do not believe that the information you requested is commercially confidential; although a confidentiality clause does cover some aspects of the contract, this was not the correct response. I believe that more clarification should have been requested from you in order to establish precisely what you were asking for.

In dealing with your request for a review, I have concentrated on the question you raised in emails to me on December 14 2010 and February 9 2011. You made it clear that the information you wanted was about where waste goes once it has been collected from NHS Manchester. I have consulted our Facilities department, and they have given me a clear explanation of what information we hold. On this basis, I believe that you should have received a clear response that we do not hold information that you have requested. I believe that the original refusal was based on a mistaken belief that all information relevant to the contract is confidential. The specific issue you asked about is not confidential. However, I do not believe that we hold the detail that you have asked for, especially given the clarity of your contact with me on the above dates.

The position is this. Once we have transferred our waste to the contractor, they have no legal or contractual obligation to tell us which location they use and do not provide this information to us. Therefore for the period in question, we do not have the exact locations to which our waste was transferred. The list of potential locations that the contractor can use is detailed below:

Bagnall and Morris Transfer Station *(SPECIFICALLY REFERRED TO ON THE 2009*
Dock Road South, *CERTIFICATE AS THIS WAS THEIR ONLY*
Bromborough, Wirral. *TIP AT THIS TIME)*
CH62 4SQ

Bagnall and Morris Transfer Station *(DID NOT OPEN UNTIL SPRING 2010. THE*
1 Europa Park *PERMIT WAS AUTHORISED BY THE*
Trafford Park *ENVIRONMENT AGENCY 22nd MARCH 2010)*
Manchester
M17 1DW

Orchid Environmental *(RECYCLING ALREADY CONFIRMED AS*
Huyton *ONLY AROUND 8%)*
Liverpool
L36 6LF

Colliers Transfer Station *(100% LANDFILL)*
Nash Road
Trafford Park
Manchester
M17 1SX

51

Viridor Transfer Station	*(95% LANDFILL AT THE TIME IN*
Trafford Wharf Road	*QUESTION)*
Manchester	
M17 1BS	
Junction 25	*(NOT OPENED UNTIL JUNE 2010)*
Ashton Road	
Bredbury	
Stockport	
SK6 2QE	
CEW	*(SPECIFICALLY DEALS WITH BUILDING*
Merton Street	*MATERIALS AND PURE SORTED*
St Helens	*COMMODITIES)*
WA9 1HU	

On this basis, the outcome of my internal review is that I can confirm that there is provision for recycling in our waste contract but the contract does not identify the levels that must be achieved. We do not hold information about what happens to waste once it has been collected.

I hope this answers the issues that you raised in your request for an internal review. I should stress that FOI and EIR only cover information that is held, and does not cover information held by other organisations. Although you clearly believe that NHS Manchester ought to hold more information about recycling, this is not covered by the FOI Act or the Environmental Information Regulations. Both pieces of legislation give you a right to the information we actually hold at the time your request is received. They do not require us to obtain information from a third party. I understand that the contract does not place specific requirements on the contractor to inform us what happens to waste, and so I do not believe that information about this, but which is held by the contractor is held for our purposes.

If there is other information that you would like to request, please let me know. If you think that there is an element of your original request that I have not considered, please let me know.

If you are unhappy with this response, you can complain to the Information Commissioner's Office. They can be contacted through the following hyperlink https://www.ico.gov.uk/Global/ contact_us.aspx.

Regards

Tim Turner

Tim Turner
Information Governance Manager
NHS Manchester'

Regarding NHS Manchester PCT's 2009 recycling certificate, my comments show it is quite easy to rule out a number of the tips listed in Mr Turner's email as open to B&M. Based on the information provided, we can conclude that NHS Manchester PCT's waste went to Bromborough, Orchid Environmental, Viridor or Collliers. However, only B&M's Bromborough site sixty miles away from Manchester could make the 2009 recycling certificate even remotely authentic. And putting Mr Kevan's testimonial, which was used to attract other clients for B&M, next to the 2009 recycling certificate does not look good for the NHS.

It took me almost seven months to obtain a copy of NHS Manchester PCT's recycling certificate under the Freedom of Information Act. When I finally received it from Mr Tim Turner on 15 April 2011, I emailed back to thank him. The response from his email box simply read:

> '*Tim Turner has now left NHS Manchester.*'

Chapter 7

The final defamation letter

'The third and final strand of our civil liberties agenda is about openness, about scrutiny. Free citizens must be able to hold big institutions and powerful individuals to account. And not only the Government. There are a whole range of organisations who, for example, benefit from public money and whose activities have a profound impact on the public good, yet who cannot be properly scrutinized. Citizens must know what goes on in these institutions. And they must be at liberty to speak out about the things they discover.'

Nick Clegg, Liberal Party Manifesto 2010

The final defamation letter came out of the blue, and I was surprised to see that it appeared to be an abuse of another of NHS Manchester PCT's written policies. The document I am referring to is called *'Raising concerns under the Public Interest Disclosure Act 1998 (Whistleblowing) policy'*, which was approved by the board in July 2009. This clearly states that *'the PCT will not tolerate the harassment or victimisation of anyone raising a genuine concern'*. The Act is there to protect freedom of enquiry into public organisations, but for some reason my genuine concern was leaked back to B&M. NHS Manchester PCT's counter fraud policy also says that *'all referrals will be treated in the strictest of confidence'*.

I was asking questions within my rights as a taxpayer under the Freedom of Information Act, but here I was with another solicitor's letter that referred to a complaint I had made to the NHS. Interestingly, the date on the letter corresponded with the removal of Peter Kevan's key testimonial on B&M's website, which stated that *'NHS Manchester can now prove our recycling figures thanks to the quarterly environmental reports'*. Why on earth would a commercial organisation take such a valuable testimonial off their website if it was true?

By now, I was used to B&M's robust legal correspondence and this last letter was, to say the least, interesting. Again, I was accused of having a *'reckless disregard for the truth'* and told I was *'actuated by malice'*. However, a new and additional claim now entered the equation, accusing me of trying to induce a breach of contract. This is an odd accusation when all I was doing was evaluating B&M's own information, which they had lodged with the government and which was freely available under the Freedom of Information Act, against the recycling certificates that had been issued to numerous organisations in Manchester including the NHS. Any reasonable person would probably draw the same conclusion as I did. What I didn't understand was that this was just another letter saying the same things as before, so why didn't they follow through on their threats if I wasn't telling the truth? Once again, the claims against STE Waste would be substantial.

The letter also accused me of involving other organisations in the dispute, but it wasn't my fault that several other companies knew exactly how B&M's business model worked and were just as unimpressed as I was at being unable to compete. Also, is it really such a crime to campaign for positive environmental change in an industry that has descended into a shambles?

I did take offence at one paragraph in this letter as I don't think it belongs in a democratic society. When a British solicitor, authorised by his client, questions an individual's dealings with an elected MP, which is none of anyone else's business, this has major implications for freedom of speech and enquiry. The letter said that '. . . *our client is also aware of one telephone call made by John Leech MP, plainly acting on information provided to him by you, concerning your allegations on the question of our client's published recycling figures. Mr Leech spoke with a manager at a NHS customer of our client and asserted that our client was* "not recycling any waste collected in Manchester and that the trading standards are currently investigating the case" *which Mr Leech went on to say he believed to be a criminal matter*'.

So, according to B&Ms solicitor, it warrants a severely threatening defamation letter when I am simply asking my MP to delve into matters that concern his coalition government regarding the taxpayer-funded NHS. I took this up with John Leech MP because, as can be seen from the above quote by his leader Nick Clegg, this issue is a cornerstone of liberal politics. I never got an explanation, merely an email saying '*Thanks for tipping me off*'. I do not know whether John Leech MP of the Liberal Democrats also received a letter threatening defamation law.

Sadly, I now felt the need to raise another complaint about the way British solicitors conduct themselves. The Solicitors Regulation Authority showed no interest, but the Legal Complaints Service replied with this email that put my mind at rest.

> '*Thank you for your enquiry.*
>
> *We hope that it will be helpful if we briefly outline our powers. The Legal Complaints Service considers the service which solicitors provide to their clients if the complaint is raised by the client in question. We are unable to give legal advice.*
>
> *If you raise an issue about someone else's solicitor we may pass your concerns to the Solicitors Regulation Authority. If a finding of professional misconduct is made, we can consider applying disciplinary sanctions against the solicitor in question, and in the most serious cases can refer the matter to the Solicitors Disciplinary Tribunal. A finding of professional misconduct does not in itself give rise to an award of compensation.*
>
> *Whilst we can consider complaints about the overall service provided, we are not able to consider complaints about the advice given by a solicitor. Nor are we able to question the way that a solicitor chose to represent a client, or whether a certain course of action was in the client's best interests. Offering an opinion on such matters would in effect amount to legal advice as to how the case should have been conducted, which is not our function.*
>
> *I understand that the firm acts for another party in this matter. I can confirm that solicitors are obliged to act in the best interests of their own clients and to follow their instructions. If*

the firm does not do so, it is open to the client to complain. A solicitor is entitled to rely on the instructions that they are given by their client and, as long as they do not know that they are false or untrue, they have no obligation to apply a pre-trial screen to establish the truthfulness of any instructions.

It therefore follows that we are unable to consider the way in which the firm chooses to represent their client. If the matter does go to Court and the Court makes any criticisms of the solicitor's conduct in conducting the matter before it, please contact this office again and the matter can be reconsidered in the light of any criticism that has been made.

If you have any further queries, you may wish to contact the Legal Complaints Helpline on 0845 6086565 and speak with one of our helpline agents. Our lines are open between 9 am and 5 pm Monday to Friday. Please note calls may be monitored/recorded for training purposes.'

So it appears that the Legal Complaints Service correctly vindicates solicitors who can, in fact, say anything to a member of the public provided they are acting in the best interests of the client who is giving them the information and authorising the letters to be sent. What is in the Public's interest is a grey area and one which must be fought over in a court of law. As far as I know, B&M's solicitor had no reason to think their client was not telling the truth as they were merely acting on instructions. A solicitor's job is to protect his client in any way he sees fit, not to consider whether they are innocent or guilty, and apparently this includes the threat of defamation when a constituent is merely asking an elected UK MP to raise questions about an environmental issue involving government procurement. Presumably if this matter ever went to court, John Leech MP from the Liberal Democrats party would also be in the dock for daring to ask questions.

I would therefore like to take this opportunity to apologise profusely to B&M's legal team as it seems they were only doing their job within the clear boundaries (or arguably lack of them) set down by their profession. I now bitterly regret all my rants on how British solicitors handle themselves as I am clearly misguided and muddled. In this instance it looks like I am out of my depth in criticising esteemed professionals who are just doing their job. In fairness to their lead solicitor, he acknowledged his error in a later email not authorised by B&M in which he said: *'You are perfectly entitled to refer any concerns to your local MP and it is also entirely proper for him to raise legitimate questions on your behalf. There is no question of trying to infringe anybody's right to free speech.'* I would obviously never dare to accuse a defamation lawyer of contradiction for fear of stressful and expensive retribution.

However, I do have a limited understanding of the law in that I know it is a constantly changing and evolving document which people power can ultimately change. For example, 100 years ago women had no voting rights, and 50 years ago it was illegal to be a homosexual in the UK. My argument here is that the environment is part of scientific study so it must be open for people to investigate evidence and make their opinions public, even if that involves criticising certain organisations and individuals. If it isn't, and if the law puts a barrier in the way of environmental protection and science-based examination, then we are on a very slippery slope for the future.

The stakes are well laid out in all the solicitor's letters and emails I received: 'Dare to ask questions and we'll take you to the cleaners'.

However, the tide is starting to change regarding science-based comments. The best example is the recent case of The British Chiropractic Association Vs Dr Singh where

Lord Judge, the Lord Chief Justice, when giving the judgment, said the court adopted the comment of Judge Easterbrook, now Chief Judge of the US Seventh Circuit Court of Appeals, who had said in Underwager v Salter, a libel action over a scientific controversy, that plaintiffs '. . . *cannot, by simply filing suit and crying "character assassination!", silence those who hold divergent views, no matter how adverse those views may be to plaintiffs' interests. Scientific controversies must be settled by the methods of science rather than by the methods of litigation . . . More papers, more discussion, better data, and more satisfactory models—not larger awards of damages—mark the path towards superior understanding of the world around us".'

(Source: The Independent newspaper)

Surely it is better for someone to raise an issue for debate and be proved wrong than be prevented from raising it at all. For the record, no one has yet given me any evidence to suggest my claims are wrong.

Indeed, with regards to scientific enquiry, all anyone has to do is show me evidence that I am wrong and I will shake their hand and apologise. I think the point has now been made that the threat of defamation law is always an unwelcome guest at any scientific investigation party, and the Defamation Law Act needs overhauling in the interests of freedom to enquire. In 2011 this draconian law is, in my own opinion, not fit for purpose. Rightly or wrongly, I believe this view is shared by most of my countrymen because I have the impression that even the legal fraternity do not fully understand it, but are quite happy to debate it in the High Court at an outrageous hourly rate.

The government's latest views on freedom of speech are set out in the below Ministerial Foreword for the new draft Defamation Bill, now closed for consultation. The only change I would like to see is to allow television cameras into UK defamation and libel court rooms, particularly where the defence of libel is a matter of public interest. In such cases, I am not sure there can be a fair trial unless the whole of the general public has access to what is being said and argued.

'Ministerial Foreword

By The Rt Hon Kenneth Clarke QC MP, Lord Chancellor and Secretary of State for Justice, and Lord McNally, Minister of State

The right to freedom of speech is a cornerstone of our constitution. It is essential to the health of our democracy that people should be free to debate issues and challenge authority—in all spheres of life, whether political, scientific, academic or any other. But freedom of speech does not mean that people should be able to ride roughshod over the reputations of others, and our defamation laws must therefore strike the right balance—between protection of freedom of speech on the one hand and protection of reputation on the other.

There has been mounting concern over the past few years that our defamation laws are not striking the right balance, but rather are having a chilling effect on freedom of speech. This is particularly important for the Coalition Government which is committed to empowering the citizen so that those in authority are held properly to account. But, as reflected in the manifestos of all three parties prior to the General Election, the consensus for reform goes much wider than this.

We are pleased to be able to publish the Government's proposals for reform of the law on defamation for public consultation and pre-legislative scrutiny. Our core aim in preparing these provisions has been to ensure that the balance referred to above is achieved, so that people who have been defamed are able to take action to protect their reputation where appropriate, but so that free speech and freedom of expression are not unjustifiably impeded by actual or threatened libel proceedings.

We are particularly concerned to ensure that the threat of libel proceedings is not used to frustrate robust scientific and academic debate, or to impede responsible investigative journalism and the valuable work undertaken by nongovernmental organisations. We also wish to reduce the potential for trivial or unfounded claims and address the perception that our courts are an attractive forum for libel claimants with little connection to this country, so that our law is respected internationally.

The draft Bill does not directly deal with issues relating to costs in defamation proceedings. However, a fundamental concern underlying these reforms is to simplify and clarify the law and procedures to help reduce the length of proceedings and the substantial costs that can arise. The proposals that the Government intends to take forward subject to the results of our recent consultation on Lord Justice Jackson's proposals for reform of civil litigation funding and costs including conditional fee agreements will have a significant impact on reducing costs in civil proceedings generally, and proposals which will shortly be put forward in relation to civil justice reform will encourage and promote alternative dispute resolution and settlement. In addition, this paper consults on proposals for a new procedure to resolve key issues in defamation proceedings at an early stage to encourage settlement and prevent protracted and costly litigation, and the draft Bill proposes the removal of the presumption in favour of jury trial in defamation cases, which currently acts as an impediment to the early resolution of issues, so that the courts will have a discretion to provide for jury trials where this is in the interests of justice.

The law on defamation has evolved over a considerable period of time and is still largely a matter of common law. Because of this, there are inevitably risks in trying to encapsulate key elements of the law in statute in an area where extensive case law already exists. In formulating the proposals in the draft Bill we have been very conscious of the need to articulate key provisions in a way which is as simple and easy to understand and apply as possible, in order to avoid generating further uncertainty and litigation. We would very much welcome views on whether the draft Bill achieves this and manages to strike the right balance between the competing interests involved.

In publishing the draft Bill we would in particular like to record our appreciation of the contribution made by Lord Lester of Herne Hill to the debate on these important issues, both through his own Private Member's Bill on the subject and through the valuable assistance that he and his expert team (Sir Brian Neill and Heather Rogers QC) have given to our considerations. We believe that the detailed attention which the draft Bill and other consultation proposals will receive through the public consultation and pre-legislative scrutiny process represents an effective approach which will enable us to achieve fully considered legislative proposals which focus on core issues of concern where legislation can make a real difference. We look forward to a healthy debate, and encourage all those with an interest to take part.

Kenneth Clarke Lord McNally
Lord Chancellor and Minister of State
Secretary of State for Justice'

To return to my communications with B&M's solicitors, a few more emails were exchanged and in the end, I decided to play a few cards and share some of the government information with them. This obviously did the trick as the next day a person came to my reception area and asked to see me without an appointment. The person was none other than Ken Curtis, the big cheese of B&M.

Most people get offered a cup of tea and a chocolate biscuit when they come into my domain. But given the threatening correspondence this gentleman had authorised, there was no chance of any red carpet treatment here. Perhaps the most bizarre part of this whole story is that when the multi millionaire Mr Curtis turned up at my office, I actually felt sorry for him. If the circumstances had been different, I may actually have warmed to him. He acted very sheepishly throughout the meeting and told me he expected to be fined over my complaint. For the first time in this whole debacle, the two parties were in complete agreement. Anyone who holds their hands up and admits they are in the wrong and are willing to accept the consequences cannot be asked to do anything else.

However, Mr Curtis did make one of the most ridiculous comments I have ever heard about the waste industry. By this time he knew I had followed his trucks again after I had been tipped off that they were taking their waste directly to the Viridor landfill site in Pillsworth, on the outskirts of Manchester. He said this practice had now stopped after Viridor had refused to give him recycling certificates for his activities. Only Viridor's representatives will know if this ludicrous conversation ever took place, but it seems odd that a FTSE 100 company would entertain such a request. He refused to discuss the issue of his own 95% recycling certificates apart from the fact that they had '*changed format*' due to my complaint. Mr Curtis also offered to subcontract back the work he had taken off me, but I declined his offer.

At the end of this short meeting, we both agreed to put the guns down until Trading Standards reported back.

Chapter 8

The Trading Standards report

'When people agree with me, I always feel I must be wrong.'

Oscar Wilde

In late September Peter Duffin called to tell me that a facilities management company had agreed to give a witness statement saying they had been deceived by B&M's recycling certificates. However, by October it had become obvious the company had changed its mind. I still don't know who they were or why they pulled out of the legal process, but on 4 October, Peter Duffin told me the whole case now hinged on NHS Manchester PCT's recycling certificates.

On 14 October 2010, Neil Geddes confirmed Manchester Trading Standards' position to me by email:

> *'If it can be shown that there is evidence to link the Recycling Reports, the Environment Agency Returns and the NHS Contract and that there was a fraudulent act committed then we will be recommending to "legal" to raise criminal proceedings against the perpetrator.'*

So it came as no surprise when, on 3 November 2010, Trading Standards finally reported back to me as follows:

> *'Date: 3 November 2010*
> *Our Ref: C36745*
>
> *Dear Mr. Farmer,*
>
> *I write further to your complaint received by Manchester City Council's Trading Standards Service on 6 May 2010.*
>
> *The complaint was against Bagnall & Morris (Waste Services) Ltd, c/o McEwan Wallace, 68 Argyle Street, Birkenhead, Wirral CH41 6AF and the basis of your complaint was that:*
>
> - *"Bagnall and Morris have a £5 million operation in Manchester which involves hospitals such as Christies and Hope, top 100 companies etc. and they are giving out certificates which claim 95% recycling in Manchester.*
> - *They have been recycling none of it and have been taking it to sites that do not recycle".*

During the initial investigations into this complaint it became clear that Manchester Trading Standards would need to contact other local authority Trading Standards Services and the Environment Agency as the issue was complex and appeared to have an impact in a number of local authorities. To that end a joint meeting with these other agencies was held on 20 May 2010 at the offices of the Environment Agency in Warrington.

Following this meeting Manchester Trading Standards began making enquiries in relation to the recycling claims made by Bagnall & Morris and started to gather evidence to support your allegations.

A number of documents were provided to us from the Environment Agency and yourself, which were studied at length, along with a myriad of communications from you providing additional information and suggestions you thought would be of use in this investigation.

At the beginning of June 2010 the investigation was discussed with our Legal Services. At this time we thought that the complaint could have been considered under either:

    1.   Business Protection from Misleading Marketing Regulations 2008 SI No. 1276, or
    2.   The Fraud Act 2006.

However, at this time we did not have sufficient evidence to support any alleged criminal offences.

We also contacted Greater Manchester Police Economic Crime Section in relation to a possible fraud, however they felt that if there were any false claims in marketing materials then this would fall within the remit of Trading Standards.

In order to assist our understanding of the exact nature of the complaint we asked for support from Manchester Waste Management Services who were able to make the whole issue clearer to us. As a result it became evident that the recycling reports issued by Bagnall & Morris to their various clients and the Environment Agency Quarterly Returns produced by Bagnall & Morris for their Bromborough facility were at odds with each other. In at least one quarterly report to the Environment Agency Bagnall & Morris had sent over 60% of the waste received at Bromborough to landfill yet none of the waste actually came from Manchester, similar reports showed 30-40% of waste going to landfill. Yet they claimed circa 95% recycling efficiency in the recycling reports.

On 22 June 2010 you gave Mr. Duffin your statement and we received a copy of your duly signed completed statement on 1 July 2010.

Following further communications from yourself I responded to you on the 24 June 2010 again making clear the nature of our investigation. We planned to speak to various clients of Bagnall & Morris to establish whether we could obtain sufficient evidence to prove the recycling reports deceived them and affected their economic behaviour. Without such evidence we would be unable to support a successful prosecution.

During July 2010 Mr. Duffin contacted various clients of Bagnall & Morris in Central Manchester whose details had been provided by you.

A number of visits were arranged and your allegations against Bagnall & Morris were discussed at length. Unfortunately none of the parties interviewed would provide a statement indicating that they were deceived by the recycling reports issued to them by Bagnall & Morris nor that the recycling reports had affected their economic behaviour.

During this period, July 2010, we requested formal statements from the Environment Agency to support the Environment Agency Quarterly Returns provided by Bagnall and Morris. The signed statements were subsequently received on 7 September 2010.

On 22 September 2010 representatives of Bagnall & Morris were interviewed under caution following Police and Criminal Evidence Act guidance.

Following this further discussions were held with Manchester City Council's Legal Services. It was agreed that a further approach would be made to Manchester Primary Care Trust to determine whether or not the recycling reports provided by Bagnall & Morris or the fact their waste did not go to Bromborough had affected their economic behaviour in awarding their waste contract to Bagnall & Morris—we were advised they did not, nor were either the recycling reports or where the waste was to be sent included in the contract.

Therefore I must conclude, that having been unable to link the recycling reports provided by Bagnall & Morris to having affected their client's economic behaviour, we are unable to prove any alleged offences under either:

1. *The Business Protection from Misleading Marketing Regulations 2008 SI No. 1276, or*
2. *The Fraud Act 2006.*

I appreciate that you will be disappointed with this outcome; however I can assure you that we have taken all the necessary steps to try to meet the required evidential standards to prove this matter.
If there are any matters in this letter on which you seek further clarification do not hesitate to contact me.

Yours sincerely

Neil Geddes
Principal Trading Standards Specialist'

The key sentence in the report is this one: '*Unfortunately none of the parties interviewed would provide a statement indicating that they were deceived by the recycling reports issued to them by Bagnall and Morris nor that the recycling reports had affected their economic behaviour.*' Why does Mr Geddes use the word 'unfortunately'? The Concise Oxford Dictionary's definition of this word is '*having bad fortune, unlucky, regrettable or inappropriate*'.

When I spoke to Mr Geddes about the report, he said '*That* (meaning my complaint) *should never have been on my desk*'. Mr Duffin went one better when he told me that '*he hates been laughed at*'. I got the impression, rightly or wrongly, that Mr Geddes and Mr Duffin were both uneasy with the final Trading Standards report. And it has crossed my mind that other forces may have been at work here, given the fact that this issue and its timing would have been a political disaster for Manchester City Council due to their Labour Party bias. However, this book is about a critique of the evidence rather than the politics of conspiracy, so back to the report.

In my opinion, Trading Standards couldn't get anyone to give a witness statement because they were talking to the wrong people, i.e. the facilities management companies. It was a serious mistake not to talk to the tenants of the buildings in question. It is the tenants who pay rent and keep the commercial property market and economy afloat in Manchester, but they were seen as irrelevant to the investigation. However, under UK duty of care law relating to the waste industry, it is the tenants who have legal ownership of the waste because they create it. The facilities management companies are merely agents working for landlords who select a waste company on behalf of all the tenants in their buildings.

These same tenants also employ environment officers to cover their corporate and social responsibilities and to ensure their organisations are fulfilling their financial reporting requirements as well as making green marketing statements. The tenants need the recycling certificates to make their corporate and social responsibility claims, so not to consult them therefore makes the investigation look flawed as it is they who ultimately bare the cost and decide whether or not recycling performance is linked to economic behaviour. However, it is easy to see why Manchester Trading Standards, with their lack of resources, did not go further than talking to the facilities management companies.

The report confirms that these facilities management companies had certificates citing a recycling efficiency rate of around 95%, yet none of the waste actually went to B&M's Bromborough recycling station. In an email quoted in Chapter 5, we saw that Neil Geddes fully understood the audit trail and acknowledged that the certificates and B&M website testimonials (falsely) related to the Bromborough site. But as no one was willing to provide a witness statement to this effect, the case simply fell apart as under the laws Trading Standards were using, they had to prove the certificates affected economic behaviour. And if they could not prove this with witness statements, it did not matter whether or not the certificates were false. The audit trails and tipping totals for the Viridor and Colliers waste treatment plants provided by John Christey from the Environment Agency were, for some reason, seen as irrelevant—which is remarkable as this evidence proves B&M were using tips in Manchester that did very little commercial recycling.

I do not have the exact figures for the tonnage of commercial waste that B&M collected from Manchester and tipped at Colliers and Viridor, but I can estimate them based on the observational evidence collected by STE Waste during January 2010. The estimated figure for March 2009 to March 2010 is in the tens of thousands of tonnes. Pennon, which owns Viridor, is a FTSE 100 company and will hold the actual records of B&M's tipping for the period in question for a few years to come. Colliers will need to hold the same records until at least 2013.

As a result, Manchester Trading Standards is the only organisation I know of that cannot link recycling to the economic business decision of purchasing waste services. I think that most of the tenants who pay rent in Manchester and make environmental statements on their websites based on recycling claims will find this fact alarming—particularly as they weren't even given the chance to contribute to the debate on whether recycling percentages are linked to their economic behaviour.

I took up Mr Geddes' offer to seek further clarification and sent him a number of questions. These were kindly answered by his line manager Ms Janet Shaw, the Specialist Services Manager for Manchester Trading Standards.

'Dear Mr Farmer,

Request for Information—Complaint about Bagnall & Morris—Ref ENV/8AZL22

Thank you for your request for information, which was received by Manchester City Council on 4 November, and has been considered under the provisions of the Freedom of Information Act 2000.

I confirm that the Council does hold some of the information that you have requested. However, having carefully considered the information, the Council has determined that it is unable to comply with part of your request. This is because part of the requested information is exempt from disclosure under the following qualified exemptions:

Section 21—Information accessible to applicant by other means
Section 30—Investigations and proceedings conducted by public authorities
Section 40—Personal Information

I have indicated in the response to the questions below when each of these exemptions applies.

In response to your request, I am able to provide the following answers to the questions raised:

1. Which other local authority Trading Standards were involved?

Trafford and Wirral Trading Standards—as your complaint referred to businesses based in these authorities.

2. Please can I have a copy of the minutes of the meeting that took place in Warrington on 20th May, 2010?

No minutes were taken during the meeting.

3. Was the lack of sufficient evidence in June down to the fact that you did not have witness statements from clients of Bagnall & Morris to support the allegation?

Partly, but we also did not have a statement from the Environment Agency confirming the records they held in respect of B & M's Environment Agency Waste Returns.

4. Why did you contact the Greater Manchester Police Economic Crime Section?

As detailed in the outcome letter sent to you on 3 November, 2010, we contacted them in relation to a possible fraud.

5. Who is the person(s) at Manchester Waste Management Services who made the whole picture a lot clearer? Please can I have a copy of their correspondence with yourselves?

This information is exempt information under the Freedom of Information Act, 2000, Section 40(2) and cannot be disclosed.

6. Can you confirm that you agree that the recycling reports issued by B & M are false? This is how I am reading the paragraph in the middle of the second page of the report because presumably you would have shut the case down at that point if there had been any doubt they were true?

We cannot say the recycling reports are false. What we can say is that they are at odds with the information provided by B & M to the Environment Agency in their quarterly Waste Returns. You have already received the relevant periods' B & M Waste Returns from the Environment Agency and you know the figures cannot be reconciled. We cannot say which of these documents are incorrect.

7. What questions did you ask the facilities managers? Please can I have a copy of the list of questions and the names of the people and their companies that you went to see? I gave you the list so presumably you can tell me who you went to see.

This information is exempt information under the Freedom of Information Act, 2000, Section 30, and cannot be disclosed.

8. Are you aware that these people are not actually the clients here because they only facilitate. The client is actually all the tenants and/or the owner of the building. The facilities managers should not really be answering the questions here about the recycling reports as they have the most to lose if they are deemed to be false.

We are aware that the facilities managers are not the direct clients. However, we disagree with your assertion that the facilities managers should not be answering our questions as we understand they manage the building on behalf of all the tenants and therefore engage one waste management firm to deal with the building's waste.

9. How many actual building tenants did you ask if they were bothered that the recycling certificates may be false? The Royal Bank of Scotland for example rather than ISS who only manage their buildings. Please take another look at the ISS letter that I gave you in the witness statement because this is clearly at odds with what you are saying here.

None, as we concluded that the facilities manager could speak on behalf of the building.

10. Were the facilities management companies asked to provide a statement?

They were interviewed as part of the investigation. We cannot disclose whether individual facilities managers provided a statement as this is exempt information under the Freedom of Information Act, 2000, Section 30.

11. Can I conclude from this that the fact that the certificates are false has no bearing on any of them to use Bagnall & Morris? In other words the certificates are deemed irrelevant.

We cannot comment on the judgements that may or not have been made by the facilities managers.

12. Can you confirm that the Manchester PCT was not bothered where their waste went or whether or not it was recycled because it was not in the contract?

We cannot disclose what opinions may have been given by representatives of Manchester PCT. This is exempt information under the Freedom of Information Act, 2000, Section 30.

13. Was David McGarrigan or anyone else asked about Peter Kevan's testimonial endorsement regarding recycling reports on B & M's website? What was the reply?

This is exempt information under the Freedom of Information Act, 2000, Section 30, and cannot be disclosed.

14. If Manchester NHS PCT had provision for recycling in their contract would you have recommended a prosecution? You say in previous emails that you would have.

We have already answered this in the outcome letter when we say 'that having been unable to link the recycling reports provided by Bagnall & Morris to having affected their client's economic behaviour, that we are unable to prove any alleged offences'. If we had there is a strong possibility we would have submitted a prosecution report to our legal services section recommending such action.

15. Please can I have a CD copy of the Bagnall and Morris interview for my own legal people?

No, this is exempt information under the Freedom of Information Act, 2000, Section 30 and cannot be disclosed.

16. Please can I have the totals tipped by Bagnall and Morris in Viridor and Colliers that were given to you by John Christey?

No, this is exempt information under the Freedom of Information Act, 2000, Section 21 as this information is reasonably accessible to you by requesting it from the Environment Agency.

17. Can you confirm that I was correct or incorrect in my allegations but this fact is irrelevant because there has been no financial fraud?

See response to questions 6 and 14 above.

18. Can you confirm what environmental/green economy legislation you had at your disposal to help you with this case?

No specific environmental/green economy legislation was available for us to use to investigate your complaint. We were seeking to use the Business Protection from Misleading Marketing Regulations, 2008, and the Fraud Act, 2006.'

Once again, Manchester Trading Standards confirm in their answer to question 14 that there was a '*strong possibility*' they would have recommended a prosecution if they could have linked the recycling certificates to economic behaviour. They also confirm they had no environmental or green economy legislation to refer to during the investigation.

Ms Shaw's email shows that Trading Standards agree that the facilities management companies are not B&M's direct clients. But the big question is: if recycling certificates aren't important, why do they exist and why do clients ask for them? The Biffa email reproduced in Chapter 1 clearly shows the importance of recycling information to many companies that produce large amounts of waste.

However, it is the answer to question 6 that is the most interesting and the fact that this book is still in the dark as to the actual tonnage of waste tipped by B&M at Viridor and Colliers between 2006 and 2010.

At the same time as the Trading Standards report came through, I received the latest waste return information (covering the July to September 2010 period) for B&M's Bromborough site after requesting this from the Environment Agency. This is reproduced below:

Environment Agency

Waste Return

Environmental Protection Act 1990
Pollution Prevention and Control Act 1999

Date of issue:	* Use this form to tell us the type and quantity of controlled waste you have processed at each facility on your site over the last quarter.

When completed please E-Mail to:

monitoring.east@environment-agency.gov

* Please read through the whole form and guidance notes before you start filling anything in.

* Please e-mail the completed form back to us within 28 days of the end of the return period to the address on the left.

1 Return Period

Period name:	Year
Qtr Jul-Sep	2010

Landfill Sites Only

2.5 Remaining void space covered by licence

2 Operator and site details

Site Operator

Bagnall & Morris (Waste Services) Ltd

PPC Permit or WM Licence no.

50159

Site name

Bagnall & Morris (Waste Services) Ltd

Site Address

16 Dock Road South
Bromborough
Wirral

Post Code: CH62 4SQ

2.6 Was the site fully surveyed in the past 12 months?

[ ] if no go to question 2.7   Date Surveyed [ ]

How was the void space calculated?

2.7 How have you estimated the remaining void space?

For example visually or other method

2.8 Remaining life of site (Years)

Now go to sections 3 and 4 (waste received/removed from site)

2.2 Type of facility

A11 - Household, Commercial & Industrial Waste Transfer Stn

2.3 Was a weighbridge used?

	Yes
Percentage weighed	100 %

2.5 If you are not operating a landfill go to section 3

5 Declaration

I certify that the information in this return is correct to the best of my knowledge and belief.

Name	James Owen
Position	Transfer Station Manager
Phone	077920 75 984

Date 18/10/2010

6 Disclosure and data protection

The information you provide will be used by the Environment Agency to enable it to fulfil its regulatory and waste management planning responsibilities.
For full information on how the data in this form will be used please see the waste return guidance notes.

WASTE RECEIVED ON SITE

Please read the guidance notes before filling in the form

Running total (Amount)   5,576.57

Origin	EWC Waste Code	State	Amount	Units	final disposal	Used on site	Hazardous	From another facility	Bio'able Municipal	Other Bio'able
								Additional info		
Liverpool	200101	Solid	847.5	Tonnes	No	No	No	No	No	Yes
Wirral	200101	Solid	847.5	Tonnes	No	No	No	No	No	Yes
Liverpool	200138	Solid	20.95	Tonnes	No	No	No	No	No	Yes
Wirral	200138	Solid	20.95	Tonnes	No	No	No	No	No	Yes
Liverpool	200139	Solid	47.36	Tonnes	No	No	No	No	No	Yes
Wirral	200139	Solid	47.36	Tonnes	No	No	No	No	No	Yes
Liverpool	200140	Solid	13.02	Tonnes	No	No	No	No	No	Yes
Wirral	200140	Solid	13.02	Tonnes	No	No	No	No	No	Yes
Liverpool	200108	Solid	1824.46	Tonnes	No	No	No	No	No	Yes
Wirral	200108	Solid	1824.45	Tonnes	No	No	No	No	No	Yes
Liverpool	200102	Solid	35	Tonnes	No	No	No	No	No	Yes
Wirral	200102	Solid	35	Tonnes	No	No	No	No	No	Yes

WASTE REMOVED FROM SITE

Please read the guidance notes before filling in the form

Running total (Amount)   5,576.59

Destination	EWC Waste Code	State	Amount	Units	Hazardous	Destination Facility Type
Wirral	200301	Solid	3,648.91	Tonnes	No	3 - Landfill
Manchester	200101	Solid	1,208.65	Tonnes	No	5 - Reprocessing
Manchester	200101	Solid	24.89	Tonnes	No	5 - Reprocessing
Crewe & Nantwich	200101	Solid	461.47	Tonnes	No	5 - Reprocessing
Lancashire	200138	Solid	41.90	Tonnes	No	5 - Reprocessing
Wirral	200140	Solid	26.05	Tonnes	No	6 - Recycling
Manchester	200139	Solid	66.90	Tonnes	No	6 - Recycling
Manchester	200139	Solid	10.48	Tonnes	No	6 - Recycling
Liverpool	200139	Solid	9.57	Tonnes	No	6 - Recycling
Liverpool	200139	Solid	7.77	Tonnes	No	6 - Recycling
Cheshire	200102	Solid	70.00	Tonnes	No	5 - Reprocessing

After receiving the waste return, I sent the following email to Neil Geddes on 7 November:

'Neil

Following on from last week can you please confirm that you have had a look at this waste return and whether or not I am seeing things.

Technically only 2% recycling. (120 out of 5576 tonnes removed from site).

In the interests of fair trading, surely they must not be allowed to travel around Manchester with the strap line:

"Recycling led waste management".

> *Your comments please based on what you now know about the waste industry would be appreciated.*
>
> *Marcus Farmer'*

Neil sent me this reply:

> *'Marcus,*
>
> *I agree with your figures, however as Wirral are the Home Authority for Bagnall & Morris and this statement impacts not just on Manchester but includes Liverpool and all other local authorities where the vehicles work then Wirral are best placed to deal with this claim.*
>
> *I am aware that Pete has been in touch with Wirral TS regarding this matter.*
>
> *Neil*
>
> *Neil Geddes*
> *Temporary Principal Trading Standards Specialist*
> *Manchester City Council*
> *1 Hammerstone Road*
> *Gorton*
> *Manchester*
> *M18 8EQ'*

So there we have it. A principal UK Trading Standards specialist agrees that the Bromborough waste station's recycling performance is only 2%, but can't do anything about the company in question handing out recycling certificates—a crucial part of their sales literature—claiming it is 95%.

In true public sector style, and not for the first time in this story, Neil Geddes has successfully pushed the issue onto someone else's desk. At this point, I found the idea of dealing with Wirral Trading Standards and their lack of resources and understanding of the waste industry a bridge too far.

For a few days in mid November 2010, a national newspaper and well-known environmental journalist took a keen interest in the story and I was led to believe an article was written. However, I was also told the story was in a queue and its publication would depend on the number of high profile and relevant public interest stories that arose that week. On 16 November 2010, William and Kate announced they were going to be married the following April, and that was that. My preference was always to get a renowned, quality and independent journalist to raise a debate around my story, but this had now been thwarted twice by circumstances outside my control. The only person left to write the story was me.

Chapter 9

Manchester's senior politicians

'I have come to the conclusion that politics are too serious a matter to be left to the politicians.'

Charles De Gaulle

When you have a serious environmental issue that's affecting your business, I think it's fair to say that an MP who campaigns vigorously on the issue should pick up the ball and run with it—particularly if the issue involves a government-funded organisation that's paid for by the taxpayer. In the last chapter, the argument boiled down to the fact that Trading Standards were unable to link recycling to economic behaviour, but if they could have proved this link they would probably have recommended a prosecution. In many of my emails to John Leech MP I found myself battling with someone who I felt simply didn't understand the issue. I told him I felt he was missing the point about the green economy and, in particular, regarding his local NHS. This was the email exchange that followed on 4 March 2011:

> *'No Marcus, it is you that have missed the point. While I agree that the outcome is not satisfactory it has been investigated, no criminal offence has been committed because the contract was not won on the basis of claims over recycling rates. You know this, and while I share your frustration you cannot move the goalposts after the event.*
>
> *John'*

> *'John*
>
> *You 'agree that the outcome is not satisfactory' and 'you share my frustration' and it is me 'who has missed the point'.*
>
> *For your information, you can actually move the goalposts after the event. It's called campaigning for positive change which is what you are paid to do.*
>
> *Marcus Farmer'*

My argument with Mr Leech concerned a letter from Peter Akid, Chief Executive of the North West Collaborative Commercial Agency (NWCCA), which awards contracts on behalf of NHS North West. I believe this letter, reproduced below, proves that recycling played a major part in

NWCCA's supplier selection process. In other words, recycling reports for NHS North West **were** linked to the client's economic behaviour.

Commercial Procurement Solutions

Shared Business Services NHS

John Leech MP
8 Gawsworth Avenue
East Didsbury
M20 5NF

Chandlers Point
Halyard Court
31 Broadway
The Quays, Salford
M50 2UW

31 January 2011   RECEIVED 02 FEB 2011

www.sbs.nhs.uk

Dear Mr Leech

I am writing to acknowledge receipt and respond to your letter of the 24th December 2010 relating to Waste Disposal agreements utilised by NHS Trusts in the North West region, and the Christie Hospital in particular.

The original tendering process had a number of key aims and objectives set out by our customer trusts, to improve overall waste management services and practices on sites, reducing the environmental impact and volumes of waste processed.

The contractors bidding were advised of the need to provide submissions that addressed the development of waste management practices which would support effective auditing and monitoring of waste streams, and for the training, and education of key personnel, and development of management information to improve waste management activities. This undoubtedly leads to a stronger baseline understanding of existing performance levels, supporting trusts to then set progressive recycling targets aligned with those set by the NHS and Government for public sector bodies.

To this end, trusts also evaluated bidder submissions to assess their ability to effectively segregate, recycle, reuse or appropriately dispose of a range of general, domestic and hazardous materials.

Commercial Procurement Services (formerly NWCCA) has approached the Environmental Agency who have now responded formally in writing that "the local environment management team have confirmed Bagnall and Morris waste activities are legitimate, that their sites were inspected recently and met all the requirements for their permit conditions, and are not under any investigation or review by the Agency."

As such we can confirm that the service specification set out by the trust stakeholders is being met by the contracted bidder, and that their existing services and actions have been further reviewed and passed by the Environmental Agency.

I trust that the foregoing will enable you to answer your constituent query.

Yours sincerely

Peter Akid
Managing Director
NHS SBS Commercial Procurement Solutions

Mr Akid, who is ultimately responsible for vetting NHS North West's suppliers, clearly talks here about reducing environmental impact and the need to develop waste management practices which support the effective auditing and monitoring of waste streams—practices which would, I assume, include recycling certificates because they ultimately inform the NHS of their overall environmental performance with regards waste management. Mr Akid reaffirms this position when he says '. . . *to this end, trusts also evaluated bidder submissions to assess their ability to effectively segregate, recycle, reuse or appropriately dispose of a range of general, domestic and hazardous materials*'.

We can only conclude from this letter that recycling must be linked to NHS North West's economic purchasing decisions. Regarding the auditing and monitoring of waste streams, I will leave it to Mr Akid to explain why the 85% recycling rate shown on NHS Manchester PCT's 2009 certificate plummeted to just 46% in less than a year. The 2010 certificate shows a completely different waste collection method and recycling result, but in reality, the collection method hadn't changed.

Mr Akid says the Environment Agency have further reviewed and passed B&M's existing services and actions, which suggests they were happy with the certificates B&M issued to NHS North West. However, this wasn't the feedback I'd received when I met with John Christey and Gordon Whittaker at the Environment Agency eight months earlier, just before they handed my complaint over to Trading Standards. Based on the emails I received, my view was that the Environment Agency had washed their hands of the whole recycling certificates issue.

John Leech MP answered my final email about Mr Akid's letter on 5 August 2011 in the following way, pretty much summing up the current situation and state of play in the green economy. If an MP who has the power to ultimately change laws can't do anything to protect STE Waste, then who can?

> *'Your argument all along has been that B&M won the contract based on false claims of very high recycling rates. I have always argued that this would appear to have been the case, but the NHS has always denied this, while at the same time highlighting its own recycling performance. Unfortunately there appears to be little that can be done about it except what has already been done—B&M being forced to provide accurate data. In future contracts it will be far more difficult for organisations to give contracts to them based on price, because they won't be able to claim that it was the best deal for the environment in terms of recycling performance.*
>
> *John'.*

Until the new Defamation Bill has been passed, one of the main defences currently available is that of 'fair comment'. This is used if the defendant can show that their allegedly defamatory statement was simply a view that any reasonable person could have held, even if they were motivated by dislike or hatred of the plaintiff. Although I have criticised my MP here for not understanding the need to defend genuine green businesses, despite our ideological differences on a number of issues, I would not dispute the fact that he is a decent and reasonable person who works very hard for his local community. And about twenty thousand other people also seem to agree John Leech MP is a reasonable person, or they would not have voted for him at the general election. That said, the question asked of John Leech MP still remains the same. Just how are the liberal democrats as part of the coalition government going to create a green economy without laws and policies in place to protect genuine green companies?

Sir Howard Bernstein, the leader of Manchester City Council, now enters the equation. Whilst waiting for Neil Geddes's report, I became impatient for answers so I emailed Sir Howard on 25 October 2010 to ask why Trading Standards were taking so long. On 29 October, he replied with a traditional public sector holding email:

> *'Dear Mr Farmer,*
>
> *Thank you for your email of 25th October. The investigation you are referring to is extremely complex, and staff from the Trading Standards have been working with our Legal Services Section to ensure the investigation is thorough and robust. I am advised that they expect to conclude their investigation early next week and will then be in a position to provide you with a full response. I appreciate your frustration with the time it has taken to conclude the investigation but I can assure you that the nature of the case has required it.*
>
> *Sir Howard Bernstein*
> *Chief Executive*
> *Manchester City Council'*

I can think of a number of adjectives to describe the Manchester Trading Standards investigation, but neither 'thorough' nor 'robust' would be among them! Surely a *'thorough and robust'* investigation would have included at least a couple of people with a modicum of knowledge about the waste industry? And I did not understand why the issue was so complex. Trading Standards had already confirmed the existence of numerous certificates claiming 95% recycling rates; they had all the necessary information about the amounts of waste being tipped at Viridor and Colliers; and they knew that a vast amount of Manchester's commercial and NHS waste could not be accounted for by the published audit trail lodged with the Environment Agency.

I replied to Sir Howard by email on 2 November, asking why the case was so complex and how a green economy can possibly function in the city he controls unless genuine companies are protected from unfair trading. I concluded by saying that it appeared that protection for green companies was non-existent in Manchester. Mr Bernstein replied on 9 November.

> *'Dear Mr Farmer,*
>
> *I am writing in response to your latest email of 2 November regarding the complaint you made to Manchester City Council's Trading Standards Service in May 2010.*
>
> *I understand that you have now received a full response from the Trading Standards Service as to why they were unable to prove any offences under the relevant legislation, namely,*

The Business Protection from Misleading Marketing Regulations, 2008, and the Fraud Act, 2008. This legislation is designed to enable enforcement across all business sectors including businesses operating in the green economy. Our Trading Standards Service is only able to use the legislation currently on the statute books that it has been authorised to enforce. If you feel that specific legislation is needed to regulate the green economy then I would suggest that you lobby your political representatives.

You are right that establishing Manchester as a low carbon city is a priority to which both the City Council and our colleagues across Greater Manchester are committed. This is a long term process. Alongside developing a more sustainable energy strategy, retrofitting our buildings and improving transport systems and green space, our plans also recognise the need for a more sustainable approach to the management of waste and commodities. We welcome the support of organisations like yours who share this view of the City's future but the Council's ability to lead and promote these changes operates, like all its services, within the parameters set by national legislation and regulation.

In conclusion I would like to assure you that our Trading Standards Service will always do its utmost to investigate complaints of unfair trading. The Service spent a lot of time trying to obtain the evidence it needed and is disappointed that on this occasion it was not forthcoming.

Yours sincerely,

Sir Howard Bernstein
Chief Executive
Manchester City Council'

The word '*unfortunately*' had already been used in Neil Geddes's report and now I had the word '*disappointed*'. The Concise Oxford Dictionary defines '*disappointed*' as '*sad or displeased because one's hopes or expectations have not been fulfilled*'. This use of this word suggests that Trading Standards wanted to prosecute but couldn't because of a legal loophole and the lack of government green policy. I sent another email on 9 November and received this reply on 15 November:

'Dear Mr Farmer,

I can assure you that the City Council takes seriously the need to investigate and enforce, where possible, non-compliance with legislation, particularly where there is a clear economic impact. I can also assure you that the City Council takes seriously its role in ensuring the scale of change required to deliver our demanding aspirations around carbon reduction and the green agenda. I am satisfied that my officers have worked diligently and appropriately to investigate your complaints and to attempt to enforce within the available legislation. We clearly have to work within that legislation and as a result of being unable to gather the required level of evidence we could not proceed with a prosecution. I am satisfied that there is appropriate legislation in place that, with sufficient evidence, can be used to prosecute non-compliant businesses.

> *Whilst I appreciate your concerns as a businessman I cannot agree with your comments about either the green economy or the City Council's responsibilities to support it.*
>
> *Yours sincerely*
>
> *Sir Howard Bernstein*
> *Chief Executive*
> *Manchester City Council'*

In all honesty Sir Howard, how much more evidence does your trading standards team need?

So it looks like two of Manchester's most senior political figures were happy to accept the results of the Trading Standards investigation. Sir Howard is right when he says I should lobby my political representatives if I think there should be specific legislation to regulate the green economy, but I also feel his comments are totally inadequate and don't even begin to deal with the central issue. I **have** lobbied my local MP vigorously—but what can I do if he won't run with the issue (apart from asking questions) and in my opinion, doesn't understand the complexity of the questions surrounding the green economy? The only avenue left open is for me to put pen to paper and start my own campaign for positive change. This is exactly what I did in May 2010. Receiving 57 votes in the general election shows that whilst I have made a start, there is still a very long way to go.

It seems that my genuine green company and everyone who works for it have been left to perish by all those who have the power to effect change. On the subject of the environment, my view of politicians is that talk is cheap. Unfortunately, too many voters are willing to listen to political propaganda spoken by people who clearly don't understand the predicament of companies who are fighting for positive environmental change and a level playing field on which to operate. I believe this lack of understanding is the most serious challenge facing the development and success of the UK's green economy.

Chapter 10

The Freedom of Information Act

'If the facts don't fit the theory, change the facts.'

Albert Einstein

Once you have used the Freedom of Information Act (FIA) to analyse government-lodged information, you realise it is a wonderful tool and a key part of our ability to question in a democratic society. I was genuinely concerned about how Manchester's waste was being managed, and the FIA gave me the opportunity to request information and form opinions based on evidence, especially regarding the NHS. The ability to question is a fundamental part of any progressive society that considers its people to be free, and criticism must be part of its development provided it is justified and backed up with evidence. As yet, no one from Trading Standards or the Environment Agency had told me I was wrong, only that they could not prove my case in a UK court of law due to the lack of witness statements regarding economic behaviour.

In late December 2010, I heard on the grapevine that B&M were now claiming that the waste returns backing up their recycling certificates were wrong and were being amended. How can anyone produce a 95% recycling certificate and get the information backing up that certificate so spectacularly wrong? The certificates for Manchester PCT and the MEN specifically referred to the *'audited waste returns'*, but who was responsible for doing the audit?

Back in January 2010, my Business development manager, who has since been made redundant due STE's inability to be able to compete, had done a waste audit at Hope Hospital in Salford with the view of submitting a quote for their confidential shredding. While he was there, he noticed B&M's waste bins on site and asked to see the hospital's recycling certificate. The facilities manager, who said he was sceptical about the document, gave him a copy, but insisted the name be blanked out. Unfortunately, I am unable to reproduce the 94.29% copy certificate here so you will have to take my word for it that, when I requested an original copy of the certificate to enable me to write this book, its format and the information shown had completely changed. The revised certificate, which I received on 1 April 2011, is shown below:

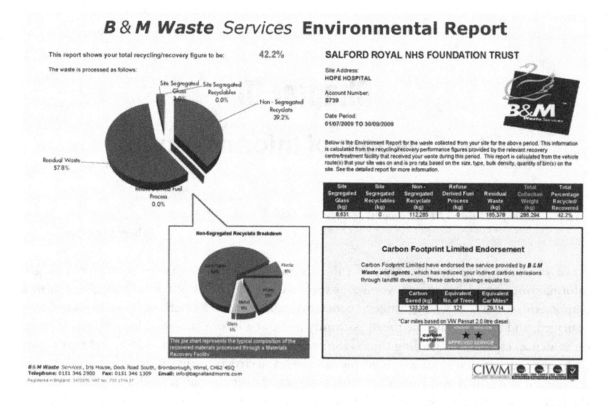

It looked to me like someone in the NHS had authorised the certificate to be changed as this was not the format used by B&M at the time. The only reason to change the original certificate would be because it was wrong. I sent an email to the Freedom of Information department at Hope Hospital asking why the certificate had been changed but as yet, I have received no reply.

The changing of government-lodged information after it has been analysed is a dangerous precedent for any investigative process, but it actually helped me in the end. People who change information and try to cover things up usually make a mistake and end up hanging themselves in the process. Mr Peter Cooke, B&M's Chief Executive, was so proud of managing to change his government-lodged information that he travelled 60 miles from Bromborough to Manchester just to tell me about it. In front of two of my staff members, he refused to admit there had been a problem in the past, almost as if I was making the whole thing up. And of course, if the facts of the complaint could be changed retrospectively there would obviously be no case to answer if anyone ever reviewed it. As a result I would then be made to look like a 'trouble causing fool'.

Regarding the certificates themselves, there is another industry, or rather administrative requirement, which has to be mentioned here—the International Organisation for Standardisation, or ISO. ISO 14001 is the badge that huge organisations wear to tell us they are environmentally sound and have the piece of paper to prove it. However, ISO, is a contradiction in terms when it comes to the UK waste industry, because there is no national policy or green law to set a standard.

Although almost laughable in the waste industry, ISO creates thousands of box ticking jobs in the UK. In the last few years I have had a number of quotes from box-ticking organisations willing to guarantee a full environmental bill of health for ISO 14001 certification—but I have yet to meet one who knows anything about the waste industry. NQA, one of the largest of these companies in the UK and one accredited by the Chartered Institute of Waste Management, is made to look foolish here as its name appears on both the original Hope Hospital recycling certificate and the revised one shown above. The NQA name also appears on the two NHS Manchester PCT recycling certificates shown earlier in the book.

The certificates that B&M gave to the MEN and the NHS state that: '*This information may be useful to support your company's environmental policy or ISO 14001 accreditation*'. This is a box-ticker's dream as it lets the company apply for ISO 14001 just by using a supplier that wears the badge. Effectively, the recycling certificate is proof—or rather plausible deniability—that an organisation has an environmentally friendly waste management system in place which allows them to make statements about corporate responsibility and green marketing. But who audits the ISO 14001 companies that hand out and authorise the badges?

The answer is: nobody. At the time of writing, there are literally hundreds of ISO certification companies operating in the UK with no qualifications to audit anything. They are all competing for the right to hand out environmental badges to organisations, and this competition often leads to a wink and a nod situation. My criticism of this box-ticking industry is that it is becoming yet another parasite on the UK economy and is preventing new entrants with fresh ideas from coming on to the market. Most innovative companies that are just starting out don't have £10,000 lying around to buy an ISO certification that then sits uselessly at the bottom of their letterhead. But it is their inability to tick this box that often prevents them from getting work and being able to compete.

It therefore stands to reason that, if there is to be a recognised ISO standard for waste management in the UK, there has to be a national standard policy. Regarding environmental management and ISO 14001, the starting point has to be a national commitment to the real recycling method, which is the most efficient way to manage waste resources. Otherwise, the whole issue is both environmentally and economically unsound. A transparent national waste policy would also provide a level playing field for everyone and organisations would no longer need to employ expensive administration to simply tick a box. If the UK is to compete and create jobs within a global green economy, I believe it must combat the expense of administration that, in many cases, produces nothing more than a green marketing illusion.

In the 1800s, Napoleon described Britain as '*une nation de boutiquiers*', which translates as 'a nation of shopkeepers'—a disparaging remark intended to portray Britain as unfit for war with France. The phrase was actually stolen from Adam Smith, the Scottish social philosopher and pioneer of the study of economics who first coined the phrase in his 1776 book 'The Wealth of Nations'. I wonder what that great man would have made of the fact that we are now 'a nation of box-tickers'.

One thing I can say for sure is that, as far as the green economy is concerned, we are unfit for war with France, Germany, China, Japan and many other international powers regarding the creation of global green jobs, simply because the UK lacks common sense around the creation of clear environmental policy.

Chapter 11

They haven't even realised! . . . .
Or have they?

'If you tell the truth, you don't have to remember anything.'

Mark Twain

When writing a book like this, you have to be crystal clear about what you are talking about. You must also make sure that the authorities have confirmed that any information and audit trails you quote are factually correct. One of the questions I asked Trading Standards after receiving their initial report wasn't actually answered until almost five months later.

This was question 6:

'Can you confirm whether you agree or disagree that the recycling reports issued by B&M are false?'

Manchester Trading Standards' reply went as follows:

'We cannot say the recycling reports are false. What we can say is that they are at odds with the information provided by B&M to the Environment Agency in their quarterly waste returns. You have already received the relevant periods for B&M's waste returns from the Environment Agency and you know the figures cannot be reconciled. We cannot say which of these documents are incorrect.'

It therefore stands to reason that if one of the documents is proved to be factually correct you can make a clear decision about the status of the other one. As already discussed, I knew B&M were changing their waste returns but I had no idea what they were going to look like. And to enable me to write this book, they had to be confirmed as factually correct after being audited by a government agency.

In March 2011, B&M's Chief Executive, Mr Peter Cooke, was asked to describe the way his company worked, after a direct request from one of his NHS clients (I was asking too many questions again). I received a letter from Mr Cook, containing the key line: '*. . . it is misleading to compare an EA* (Environment Agency) *return for a MRF* (materials recycling facility) *with a recycling report for a customer*'. As a highly qualified management accountant, Mr Cooke obviously understands simple double entry book keeping. He even hints at this fact when he says *'An Environment Agency quarterly return is simply a record of all the movements of waste in and out* *of a MRF. By definition the total tonnage brought in has to be matched with the tonnage going out'.* And once again, at the end of Mr Cooke's letter I found a direct personal threat of legal action if I continued to ask questions.

The Environment Agency confirmed the changes to B&M's waste returns on 31 March 2011:

> '*Dear Marcus*
>
> ### PUBLIC REGISTER AND ENVIRONMENTAL INFORMATION REQUEST
> **Bagnall & Morris.**
>
> *Please find attached the amended waste returns for Bagnall & Morris 50159 for 2009.*
>
> *The returns for your 2 separate emails will follow.*
>
> *Regards,*
>
> *Katie McAlinden*
> *Customer Services Officer*
> *Appleton House*
> *430 Birchwood Boulevard*
> *Birchwood*
> *Warrington*
> *WA3 7WD'*

On 19 May, I double checked again that no other changes had been made to these documents and received this reply:

> '*Hi Marcus*
>
> *I can confirm that we have received no further changes to the waste returns that were sent to you on 31 March 2011.*
>
> *Kind Regards*
>
> *Katie McAlinden*
> *Customer Services Officer'*

So I had confirmation from B&M's Chief Executive about how the company worked, and I had the new waste returns as well. However, I still needed confirmation that the amended returns were factually correct. On 18 April 2011, Nick Chesters of Wirral Trading Standards finally came out of the woodwork to complete his casework—almost five months after Neil Geddes at Manchester had thrown the case back to him. At this point, the complaint had been on Nick Chester's desk for almost 11 months in total.

By now, as information had been seen to change retrospectively, evidence of a cover up was starting to emerge. But if that was indeed the case, Wirral Trading standards certainly hadn't read the script. In answering my complaint about B&M's strap line, 'Recycling led waste management', which was referred back to him by Neil Geddes in November 2010, Nick Chesters inadvertently answered question 6 of the original complaint:

Department of Law, HR and Asset Management

Bill Norman

Director of Law, HR and Asset Management
Town Hall, Brighton Street
Wallasey, Wirral
Merseyside, CH44 8ED
DX 708630 Seacombe

Mr Marcus Farmer date 4ᵗʰ March 2010
STE Waste Management Ltd c/o Big Storage
Earl Road
Cheadle Hulme
Cheshire
SK8 6PT

date   18ᵗʰ April 2011

Dear Mr Farmer

Bagnall and Morris Waste Services Ltd (B&M)
Strap Line—'Recycling Led Waste Management'

Following the Home Authority referral we have received from Manchester Trading Standards as a result of their investigation in to the claims made by the above company, I am writing to advise you of the following.

I have recently held a meeting with two of the Directors of Bagnall and Morris in order to establish further evidence pertaining to the slogan used on their vehicles 'Recycling Led Waste Management' in line with the evidence tendered by yourself, the Environment Agency returns form dated July to September 2010.

It transpired that the original form (July to September 2010), obtained by yourself, that was submitted to the Environment Agency contained incorrect information.

Subsequent correct forms have been resubmitted to the environment agency and have now been proven to be factually correct. Evidence was sought by Trading Standards Officers and provided by B&M both at the above mentioned meeting with the Directors of B&M, and a further joint Trading Standards visit with the Environment agency, where an audit of their waste returns was carried out.

The original form submitted to the environment agency indicated that the waste was been taken to landfill in Wirral. This was not the case, as Wirral does not have a landfill site, and has not had one for the last 4 years. The environment agency has confirmed this to be true.

Based on the audit, it was clear that the waste outlined above has gone, in the first instance, to a transfer station in Tattenhall, Cheshire. Some sorting of card and paper is carried out here. Secondly, from here the waste is then transferred to a combined MRF (Materials Recovery Facility) and landfill in Shropshire where waste is processed by recycling, reprocessing or recovery.

In addition to this, it has been evidenced that other waste has been taken to the Orchid facility in Knowsley. Segregated and co-mingled waste is also taken to B&M's recycling facilities in Brombrough and at Trafford Park. I have visited Bromborough, and can confirm that only a very small percentage of processed waste is sent to another transfer station for further processing.

No waste will go directly from B&M directly to landfill. All waste is sent to facilities that either recycle, reprocess or recover prior to going to landfill. I am of the understanding that it is a legal requirement to pre-treat all waste prior to it going to landfill.

Following the audit and the meeting, I would state that there is no significant evidence to refute the strap line that B&M have printed on to their wagons and container. I.e. 'Recycling Led Waste Management'. I believe that they are making efforts to divert their waste from landfill.

Yours sincerely,

Nick Chesters
Senior Trading Standards Officer

For the purposes of this book, the only relevant part of this letter is the statement that: '*Subsequent correct forms have been resubmitted to the environment agency and have now been proven to be factually correct*'. The letter also confirms that all the government agencies involved in this investigation attended a meeting, later confirmed as being held on 8 April 2011 (15 months after the initial complaint), during which the Environment Agency audited B&M's waste returns.

In total, six waste returns dating back to March 2009 were changed. Here are the two which correspond to the recycling certificates referred to in this book, those of the Manchester Evening News and NHS Manchester.

Environment Agency

Waste Return

Environmental Protection Act 1990
Pollution Prevention and Control Act 1999

Date of issue:

When completed please E-Mail to:

monitoring.east@environment-agency.gov

* Use this form to tell us the type and quantity of controlled waste you have processed at each facility on your site over the last quarter.

* Please read through the whole form and guidance notes before you start filling anything in.

* Please e-mail the completed form back to us within 28 days of the end of the return period to the address on the left.

1 Return Period

Period name: Qtr Jan-Mar   Year 2009

2 Operator and site details

Site Operator
Bagnall & Morris (Waste Services) Ltd

PPC Permit or WM Licence no.
50159

Site name
Bagnall & Morris (Waste Services) Ltd

Site Address
16 Dock Road South
Bromborough
Wirral

Post Code: CH62 4SQ

2.2 Type of facility

A11 - Household, Commercial & Industrial Waste Transfer Stn

2.3 Was a weighbridge used?

	Yes
Percentage weighed	100 %

2.5 If you are not operating a landfill go to section 3

Landfill Sites Only

2.5 Remaining void space covered by licence

2.6 Was the site fully surveyed in the past 12 months?

if no go to question 2.7   Date Surveyed

How was the void space calculated?

2.7 How have you estimated the remaining void space?

For example visually or other method

2.8 Remaining life of site (Years)

Now go to sections 3 and 4 (waste received/removed from site)

5 Declaration

I certify that the information in this return is correct to the best of my knowledge and belief.

Name	Barry Mapp
Position	Finance Manager
Phone	0151 346 2908

Date 15/04/2009

6 Disclosure and data protection

The information you provide will be used by the Environment Agency to enable it to fulfil its regulatory and waste management planning responsibilities.
For full information on how the data in this form will be used please see the waste return guidance notes.

84

58

WASTE RECEIVED ON SITE

Running total (Amount) 2,820.02

Please read the guidance notes before filling in the form

Origin	EWC Waste Code	State	Amount	Units	Additional info					
					final disposal	Used on site	Hazardous	From another facility	Bio'able Municipal	Other Bio'able
Liverpool	200101	Solid	662.42	Tonnes	No	No	No	No	No	Yes
Wirral	200101	Solid	662.42	Tonnes	No	No	No	No	No	Yes
Liverpool	200138	Solid	31.47	Tonnes	No	No	No	No	No	Yes
Wirral	200138	Solid	31.46	Tonnes	No	No	No	No	No	Yes
Liverpool	200139	Solid	95.32	Tonnes	No	No	No	No	No	Yes
Wirral	200139	Solid	95.32	Tonnes	No	No	No	No	No	Yes
Liverpool	200140	Solid	21.65	Tonnes	No	No	No	No	No	Yes
Wirral	200140	Solid	21.65	Tonnes	No	No	No	No	No	Yes
Liverpool	200108	Solid	599.15	Tonnes	No	No	No	No	No	Yes
Wirral	200108	Solid	599.16	Tonnes	No	No	No	No	No	Yes

WASTE REMOVED FROM SITE

Running total (Amount) 2,820.02

Please read the guidance notes before filling in the form

Destination	EWC Waste Code	State	Amount	Units	Hazardous	Destination Facility Type
Wirral	200301	Solid	1,198.31	Tonnes	No	3 - Landfill
Kent	200101	Solid	278.84	Tonnes	No	5 - Reprocessing
Stockport	200101	Solid	61.58	Tonnes	No	5 - Reprocessing
Greater London	200101	Solid	779.84	Tonnes	No	5 - Reprocessing
Cheshire	200101	Solid	204.58	Tonnes	No	5 - Reprocessing
East Midlands	200139	Solid	14.65	Tonnes	No	6 - Recycling
Cheshire	200139	Solid	25.71	Tonnes	No	6 - Recycling
Cheshire	200139	Solid	11.64	Tonnes	No	6 - Recycling
Yorkshire & Humberside	200139	Solid	63.46	Tonnes	No	6 - Recycling
Outside UK	200139	Solid	63.10	Tonnes	No	6 - Recycling
Liverpool	200139	Solid	12.08	Tonnes	No	6 - Recycling
Manchester	200138	Solid	62.93	Tonnes	No	5 - Reprocessing
Wirral	200140	Solid	43.30	Tonnes	No	6 - Recycling

Environment Agency

Environmental Protection Act 1990
Pollution Prevention and Control Act 1999

Date of issue:

When completed please E-Mail to:

monitoring.east@environment-agency.gov

* Use this form to tell us the type and quantity of controlled waste you have processed at each facility on your site over the last quarter.

* Please read through the whole form and guidance notes before you start filling anything in.

* Please e-mail the completed form back to us within 28 days of the end of the return period to the address on the left.

1 Return Period

Period name:	Year
Qtr Jul-Sep	2009

2 Operator and site details

Site Operator
Bagnall & Morris (Waste Services) Ltd

PPC Permit or WM Licence no.
50159

Site name
Bagnall & Morris (Waste Services) Ltd

Site Address
16 Dock Road South
Bromborough
Wirral

Post Code: CH62 4SQ

2.2 Type of facility

A11 - Household, Commercial & Industrial Waste Transfer Stn

2.3 Was a weighbridge used?

	Yes
Percentage weighed	100 %

2.5 If you are not operating a landfill go to section 3

Landfill Sites Only

2.5 Remaining void space covered by licence

2.6 Was the site fully surveyed in the past 12 months?

if no go to question 2.7   Date Surveyed

How was the void space calculated?

2.7 How have you estimated the remaining void space?
For example visually or other method

2.8 Remaining life of site (Years)

Now go to sections 3 and 4 (waste received/removed from site)

5 Declaration

I certify that the information in this return is correct to the best of my knowledge and belief.

Name	Barry Mapp	
Position	Finance Manager	
Phone	0151 346 2908	Date 14/09/2009

6 Disclosure and data protection

The information you provide will be used by the Environment Agency to enable it to fulfil its regulatory and waste management planning responsibilities.
For full information on how the data in this form will be used please see the waste return guidance notes.

WASTE RECEIVED ON SITE

Please read the guidance notes before filling in the form

Running total (Amount) 3,018.94

Origin	EWC Waste Code	State	Amount	Units	Additional info					
					final disposal	Used on site	Hazardous	From another facility	Bio'able Municipal	Other Bio'able
Liverpool	200101	Solid	758.74	Tonnes	No	No	No	No	No	Yes
Wirral	200101	Solid	758.74	Tonnes	No	No	No	No	No	Yes
Liverpool	200138	Solid	42.79	Tonnes	No	No	No	No	No	Yes
Wirral	200138	Solid	42.79	Tonnes	No	No	No	No	No	Yes
Liverpool	200139	Solid	117.67	Tonnes	No	No	No	No	No	Yes
Wirral	200139	Solid	117.67	Tonnes	No	No	No	No	No	Yes
Liverpool	200140	Solid	18.47	Tonnes	No	No	No	No	No	Yes
Wirral	200140	Solid	18.47	Tonnes	No	No	No	No	No	Yes
Liverpool	200108	Solid	568.55	Tonnes	No	No	No	No	No	Yes
Wirral	200108	Solid	568.55	Tonnes	No	No	No	No	No	Yes
Liverpool	200102	Solid	3.25	Tonnes	No	No	No	No	No	Yes
Wirral	200102	Solid	3.25	Tonnes	No	No	No	No	No	Yes

WASTE REMOVED FROM SITE

Please read the guidance notes before filling in the form

Running total (Amount) 3,018.90

Destination	EWC Waste Code	State	Amount	Units	Hazardous	Destination Facility Type
Oswestry	200301	Solid	1,137.09	Tonnes	No	2 - Transfer Station
Ipswich	200101	Solid	83.63	Tonnes	No	5 - Reprocessing
Cheshire	200101	Solid	433.17	Tonnes	No	5 - Reprocessing
Greater London	200101	Solid	936.88	Tonnes	No	5 - Reprocessing
Stockport	200101	Solid	1.65	Tonnes	No	5 - Reprocessing
Yorkshire & Humberside	200139	Solid	27.96	Tonnes	No	6 - Recycling
Cheshire	200139	Solid	1.94	Tonnes	No	6 - Recycling
Yorkshire & Humberside	200139	Solid	68.97	Tonnes	No	6 - Recycling
Manchester	200138	Solid	85.58	Tonnes	No	5 - Reprocessing
Wirral	200140	Solid	36.93	Tonnes	No	6 - Recycling
Manchester	200101	Solid	62.14	Tonnes	No	5 - Reprocessing
Leeds	200139	Solid	4.32	Tonnes	No	6 - Recycling
Newcastle Upon Tyne	200139	Solid	12.80	Tonnes	No	6 - Recycling
Cheshire	200139	Solid	78.86	Tonnes	No	6 - Recycling
Outside UK	200139	Solid	25.62	Tonnes	No	6 - Recycling
Liverpool	200139	Solid	14.86	Tonnes	No	6 - Recycling
Wirral	200102	Solid	6.50	Tonnes	No	5 - Reprocessing

The recycling rates relating to B&M's Bromborough site are irrelevant here—it is the other side of the waste return ledger that is more important. As can be seen, when you look at the waste returns that the Environment Agency has confirmed to be factually correct, none of the waste taken to B&M's Bromborough site ever originated from Manchester. Therefore, any certificate that refers to the Bromborough site and is given to a company in Manchester is, by definition, false. The sad fact is that the Environment Agency and joint Trading Standards team probably didn't even realise it was they, not me, who confirmed the recycling certificates were false. If they did, they certainly kept quiet about it. When I raised this matter with Manchester Trading Standards they replied as follows:

> '*Dear Mr Farmer*
>
> *I have now had the opportunity to look at the letter sent to you on 18 April by Wirral Trading Standards. You have asked me to now reassess the answer you were given to question 6 in your FOIA request and give you a response of yes or no.*
>
> *Question 6 asked "Can you confirm that you agree that the recycling reports issued by B & M are false?" Our previous response was:*
>
> *"We cannot say the recycling reports are false. What we can say is that they are at odds with the information provided by B & M to the Environment Agency in their quarterly Waste Returns. You have already received the relevant periods B & M Waste Returns from the Environment Agency and you know the figures cannot be reconciled. We cannot say which of these documents are incorrect."*
>
> *The letter from Wirral Trading Standards indicates that incorrect information had been previously supplied to the Environment Agency but that they are now satisfied that the resubmitted evidence is correct. It appears to be saying that previous records had indicated waste had gone to landfill when this was not in fact the case.*
>
> *Given that Manchester Trading Standards have not been party to any auditing that has been carried out I am still not in a position to provide you with a straight yes or no answer to question 6. You were provided with a response at the time of your FOIA request that related to the investigation we had carried out based on the evidence we had before us at that time.*
>
> *I feel it's important to reiterate that the main reason we were unable to proceed further with our investigation was because we were unable to link the recycling reports provided by Bagnall & Morris to having affected their client's economic behaviour and therefore we were unable to prove offences under the Business Protection from Misleading Marketing Regulations 2008 or the Fraud Act, 2006.*
>
> *Regards*
>
> *Janet Shaw*
> *Specialist Services Manager—Trading Standards*'

In my view, this letter shows that Manchester Trading Standards were either trying to fob me off again, or they simply didn't understand the complaint. The finishing of this book was delayed due to the fact that I was waiting for the official line from the NHS. This arrived in late September 2011 (only fourteen months after I had initially brought the problem to their attention) and is shown below

Facilities Division
Baguley Clinic
Wythenshawe
Manchester
M23 1NA

Date: 22nd September 2011

Mr M Farmer
STE Waste Limited
C/O Big Storage
Earl Road
Cheadle Hulme
Cheshire
SK8 6PT

Dear Marcus

Re–Waste Management

I am writing in response to your correspondence and information relating to B&M Waste Services and to inform you of the outcome of our investigation.

Firstly I would like to thank you for the information you have provided and for raising the associated issues with the PCT. We take such allegations very seriously and have made every effort to fully investigate them in order to reach an informed conclusion based on the available evidence.

As requested in much of your correspondence, we have endeavoured to treat all information provided by both yourself and B&M in the strictest of confidence. I can assure you that we have not conveyed any information supplied by you to B&M and similarly have provided the same assurance to B&M. With that in mind, I am somewhat limited to the detail I can provide in terms of commercially confidential information provided by B&M.

It is worth noting that during the process B&M have provided open access to commercially sensitive information related to their operation's processes and business management systems. However as stated above, I am not in a position to share this from a confidentiality view point.

Our investigation process consisted of reviewing the outcomes from both the Wirral and Manchester Trading Standards investigations, Environment Agency information, the PCTs in-house waste management team audits, NHS Procurement Services (formally NWCCA) and information provided by you. We also commissioned an independent compliance audit by a specialist waste management consultancy. I am aware that you have seen some of the above.

The basis of your complaint was related to the validity of the recycling certificates issued by B&M, the disposal methods used and that B&M gained economic favour by fraudulent means. As you are aware the issue around economic favour has been fully investigated by Wirral and Manchester Trading Standards who both were unable to find any significant evidence to support this allegation. Whilst accepting their findings, as further assurance I asked my team to review these outcomes.

To assist in providing a clear outcome I have responded to each issue as follows.

Contract Award

Prior to tendering waste services the PCT had limited recycling facilities within its premises. A factor in this was the limited space we have in our buildings to provide recycling bins and the high volumes of general public attending site making it difficult to control recycling waste streams.

We asked potential suppliers to outline their proposals to ensure the PCT improved its recycling performance whilst minimising disruption to clinical services and patient care and ensuring compliance with legal requirements and associated duty of care.

We did not specify a particular method of recycling, collection or disposal as we did not want to restrict options for suppliers or indeed limit innovation. We agreed criteria for contract award based on quality, value for money, compliance with the service specification, method of collection disposal and recycling.

The Procurement Project Team undertook a detailed evaluation of the tender returns and scored each supplier based on the above criteria. Projected levels of recycling provided by suppliers was not considered as part of the scoring method as this would be difficult to compare should on site recycling bins be the proposed method as apposed to off site segregation and would in any case be difficult to prove or disprove.

The evaluation determined that B&M represented the preferred bidder and offered the most suitable solution in terms of the criteria but also in terms of minimising disruption of clinical services and space requirements on site. B&M were therefore appointed as the preferred supplier. The recycling certificates issued by B&M did not provide them with any economic advantage in terms of contract award.

This allowed the PCT to understand baseline performance levels and set progressive recycling targets in line with national guidance.

Compliance and Performance Audit

The PCT commissioned a specialist waste management consultancy to undertake a compliance audit of B&Ms waste management operations. This included detailed analysis of its operational processes, compliance with associated duty of care, monitoring and management information, including performance reporting.

B&M gave open access to all the required information and fully supported the inspection team throughout the audit process. Clearly this allowed the team to have access to, review and gain a detailed knowledge and understanding of B&Ms commercial operations and as such all information gathered is done so in the strictest of confidence, given the commercial sensitivity. I am therefore not able to provide any such information. However I can confirm that the compliance audit could find no significant failures in terms of compliance and that the management and performance reporting systems provided a reasonable level of accuracy and detail.

In terms of the recycling certificates, whilst it was found that it was difficult to fully track and understand the movement of waste and recycling performance, there was no evidence to show that B&M had attempted to give false or misleading performance information in order to achieve high recycling performance levels. During the audit and in various meetings B&M informed both the inspection team and the PCT officers of the deficiencies in terms of management information. However B&M also informed the PCT that they were in the process of implementing a new audit and performance management system in order to ensure more accurate information. This represented a significant investment from B&M and gave the PCT further assurance that B&M were committed to providing accurate performance information.

In addition to the independent compliance audit, the PCT Facilities Team carries out spot checks and duty of care audits. The audits have shown no failure to comply with the contract specification or legal requirements.

Environment Agency Returns

As you are aware, Trading Standards officers from Manchester and Wirral Trading Standards carried out investigations into your concerns in terms of the Environment Agency returns submitted by B&M. My understanding is that you have been issued with the outcome of these investigations and that they have concluded that no legal action could be taken against B&M due to lack of evidence to support such action.

It was reported by Wirral Trading Standards that their investigation had determined that the returns submitted by B&M contained inaccurate information. However this was rectified and B&M submitted new correct returns. They also determined that B&M

waste did not go directly to landfill and that they were making efforts to divert the waste from landfill.

NHS Commercial Procurement Services confirmed that the services and actions provided had been reviewed and passed by the Environment Agency.

Trading Standards Investigation

The Trading Standards from Manchester and Wirral carried out investigations into your allegations relating to potential fraud and inaccurate marketing material. I am aware that you have received the outcome of the investigation and that no evidence could be found to support such allegations. As part of the PCT audit, the audit team reviewed the investigation findings and supported the outcomes given.

ISO Registration

As part of the PCT audit, the audit team reviewed the registration and quality audits carried out by NQA against ISO 9001 and 14001. The audits show that B&M achieve a high standard of compliance and undertake exceptionally detailed monitoring of waste data.

Conclusion

Having reviewed all the available information and comments provided by all parties including your information, the investigation concludes that the PCT supports the findings of the Trading Standards investigation and whilst some inaccuracies in performance data were found, this was not done with the intent to mislead the PCT or gain any economic benefit.

I can further report that B&M made every effort to rectify such inaccuracies in a timely manner including a significant investment in a new monitoring and tracking system to provide accurate performance figures that can be verified.

It was also found that B&M ensure compliance against the required statutory and legal requirements in terms of waste management.

During this process B&M have fully supported the PCT and given access to commercially confidential information in order to provide a full picture of how they manage their operations.

The PCT dose not intend to undertake any further investigation or audits into these matters other than those required under our duty of care requirements. We will continue to monitor performance and ensure compliance with the service specification and relevant legislation. This concludes our investigation.

I hope this information assures you of the actions we have taken.

Best regards

D McGarrigan
General Manager Facilities

It would be very easy to pull this report apart based on a number of contradictions and the fact that the NHS appears to be hiding behind the Environment Agency and the Trading Standards. A request for the report undertaken by the independent specialist waste management consultancy mentioned was turned down for confidentiality reasons but it is important to note their conclusion that 'whilst it was difficult to fully track and understand the movement of waste and recycling performance there was no evidence to show that B&M had attempted to give false or misleading performance information in order to achieve high recycling performance levels' although 'some inaccuracies in performance data were found'. Evidently, the independent specialist waste management consultancy can't have put the two recycling certificates found in chapter six side by side even though this should have been their starting point. Were they actually given the one for 2009?

Interestingly, Mr McGarrigan also assures me that at no time was information regarding my complaint ever relayed back to B&M. This I find hard to believe due to the fact that I received an extremely threatening defamation law letter from B&M's legal team which specifically referred to my complaint to the NHS. At no point should a UK MP's involvement and questions on behalf of a constituent regarding a government organisation ever be passed onto a third party who is involved in the dispute. It is my view that the NHS whistle blower policy completely failed here, a fact which has major implications for the freedom of enquiry into public affairs.

In conclusion, given all this evidence, it would appear that the Environment agency, the joint trading standards team and the NHS in the North West of England find it satisfactory for commercial and government organisations in Manchester to receive misleading environmental information in order to tick boxes and make environmental marketing claims. This is despite the fact that there is significant evidence to suggest the information received is completely false. In their view, there is no case to answer, no fraud and therefore no problem because no offence has been committed.

It would appear that I was sadly deluded in my expectations of the organisations that are employed to protect the environment and fair trading, even though it has been proved beyond doubt in this book that recycling and environmental performance **are** linked to a company's economic behaviour when buying waste services. And the very idea that a company wishing to trade in a correct and moral way is finding it impossible to do so is, it seems, irrelevant. Arguably, as it stands the official position is that B&M have done nothing wrong in Manchester so STE waste is left with only two of the three options outlined in the introduction of the book. Either it accepts the situation as part of the industry and eventually goes out of business or it copies the marketing information supplied by B&M in order to compete in the green economy. Option 3, STE's chosen route has proved to be a waste of time.

The facilities management companies who received the recycling certificates but who declined the offer to link recycling to economic behaviour in the form of a witness statement may have to square this up with their tenants and their landlords. Under the current lack of green law and environmental policy, this is ultimately none of my business even though it completely contradicts every sales meeting I have ever had with any pro environmental organisation. Every facilities management company that I have ever come across claims to be pro environmental so it would stand true that recycling is of major concern in the economic decision to employ a waste management contractor. Apparently not in Manchester according to Manchester City council!

Regarding the NHS, as a taxpayer who contributes to the funding of all government-run organisations, I think I have a right to form an opinion about their waste management methods based on evidence extracted under the Freedom of Information Act. This opinion can be confined to just one sentence: unacceptable and in need of change. It would appear, based on evidence, that the government doesn't have a clue what happens to their waste once it has left the building which further underlines the need for clarity in the form of a national strategic waste policy. With regards Manchester NHS there is evidence to suggest that the waste to energy process actually takes place in Denmark. It's almost comical that a country that stuggles for trade exports pays to export ship its waste abroad so that another country can benefit from the energy created by the process. Purely in economic and environmental terms, shouldn't part of the deal be that any UK waste to energy process is for the benefit of people who live in the UK?

With regards defamation law there is a serious problem which has to be overcome for the UK green economy. Throughout this whole debacle the onus of proof that the 95% statement being banded around by B&M lies with STE Waste and not the other way around. This is unique to the UK and at no point has B&M been asked to prove their statement by the UK trading standards. In most other civilised countries in the world if you make a statement you have to be able to prove it in line with basic scientific principles. The current state of play in the UK is that commercial organisations can say anything they want regarding the environment which will no doubt lead to the collapse of any green economy if this fundamental flaw is not addressed. For any economy to succeed its consumers must always be able to trust what they are buying and be able to challenge what is being claimed.

Given this, and all the evidence reproduced in this book, I believe that the Managing Director of a genuine green company is justified in asking the question: 'What green economy?'

Chapter 12

On a personal note

'He who wields the knife never wears the crown.'

Michael Heseltine

More often than not, putting one's head above the political parapet and going against the status quo is a risky business. However, history points to the fact that it is only those that do so who succeed in forcing positive change. We only need look to the turn of the twentieth century for a key example, when many of the suffragettes, inspired by the Pankhurst sisters, endured force feeding in prisons across Britain to ultimately carry their point and win votes for women. More recently on the international stage, we have seen Nelson Mandela and Ahn Suu Kyi incarcerated for decades for their political views. Reading about such people inspires you to campaign for political change, despite the minefield you have to cross and the number of people you have to upset to make your point.

When a book like this is written, British culture often dictates the cynical view and looks for evidence of sour grapes. In defamation law, sour grapes are referred to as 'actuated by malice'. This is another grey area because it almost means that, when you feel someone has done you an injustice, you can't speak out for fear of an expensive libel law suit. As mentioned earlier, I have twice tried to get a third party to write impartially about my experiences, but both times I have run into obstacles outside my control. I the end I was the only one with all the contradictions from the various parties in an email box which had to be emptied.

To anyone who sees this book as mere promotional literature and written for self-gain, I think it is safe to say that none of the organisations I have brought into question will be knocking the door down to use STE Waste's services. Evidence of this is shown below in an email received at 1.06pm on 21st December 2010 from a Mr Gary Duke at Lambert Smith Hampton, the only person that Mr Duffin confirmed he had a meeting with, where he said

'Mr Farmer,

You have sent me several letters during the course of tghe last. In order to limit waste (quite a pertinent subject for yourself!), please do not send me any letters or emails in future'

Given the elementary spelling mistake I make the assumption that Mr Duke sent this whilst attending his staff Christmas party. The fact that the Environment Agency and the Trading standards have found 'no significant issues to prosecute' makes it entirely understandable why Mr Duke is very dismissive of a trouble maker.

95

However, I fully understand why many people will choose not to look deeper into the actual reason for writing the book—which is to start a political campaign for positive change in the green economy. All I am promoting is to do things a better way, based on evidence, but I understand you can never fight a war without doing some sort of damage to yourself. If this is the price I have to pay for highlighting a serious problem, so be it.

When running a small business, a useful starting point is to base it around the well-known and simple managerial technique of SWOT analysis. That is, analysing your Strengths, Weaknesses, Opportunities and Threats. Threats are there to be met head on, especially the biggest threat of all which is an inability to compete in your chosen market. For the record, I don't complain about losing work to competitors who genuinely come along with new machinery, techniques and approaches, and who raise the bar of competition. That simply creates a healthy and buoyant green economy. But surely when there is evidence to suggest unfair play, I should be able to exhaust every single avenue to protect my own, genuine, livelihood and those of my employees—even if I have to criticise a government investigation which I think is flawed. To do anything less would be shirking my duties as Managing Director of a genuine company and the responsibilities I have towards the people who work for me. In this particular case, I believe that ignoring these threats to my business would eventually lead to me losing my livelihood.

B&M's solicitor claimed I have a reckless disregard for the truth and my actions are brought about by malice. This is not true. I just want to speak freely, based on evidence about something I don't like the look of, and I would like to be able to put forward suggestions without being threatened with losing everything I own. Frankly, the most positive way to deal with this situation is to be open minded and civilised, and discuss all the available avenues for changing things for the better and making Manchester the UK's finest example of how to organise and run a green economy. This is a real possibility and a real opportunity.

As already discussed, I have used a basic scientific method to write this book, as shown below:

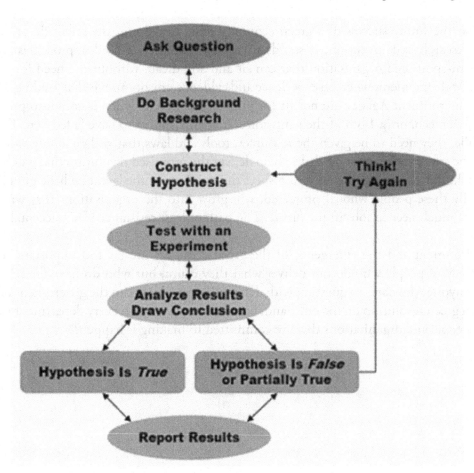

This has to be the best way to progress our society. And whilst I fully understand the nature of a tarnished reputation, the civilised approach is to offer contrary evidence to back up claims rather than get the nearest solicitor to send out threatening letters that may actually work against public interests. If anyone wants to write a response article about this book which criticises it, that's fine—as long as their conclusions are backed up with evidence. I actually welcome any positive criticism which points out clearly which bit I got wrong. I have sent numerous emails to all those involved in the case asking for evidence regarding any bits that I have missed but as yet they have all been ignored. It is my hope that this book will flush out all those different opinions based on evidence that I have not yet seen or have overlooked. Only then will the true full picture emerge.

It remains to be seen if this book will raise sufficient debate for me to claim 'job done', or whether I will have to further defend my position in the High Court in London. But what it does do is give a clear example of the strife experienced by genuine start up companies who want to operate fairly on a level playing field. The green economy is currently a very difficult place to trade because it is littered with salespeople who don't either care or don't understand what they sell and are purely motivated by the commission they earn. If millions of green collar jobs are to ever be created, the government of the day must meet this issue head on as it leads to distrust in the market place which then works against the genuine players and then ultimately the consumers.

Given that the future success of a green economy relies heavily on the scientific principles of enquiry, research and invention, it stands to reason that the civilised approach is to have a government-sponsored organisation that can sit and adjudicate without the need for expensive law suits. At the moment, based on experience and evidence, my opinion is that Trading Standards and the Environment Agency are not fit for purpose in the UK when it comes to protecting a thriving green economy. Both of their mission statements appear to have failed here. To become worthwhile, they need to be given the resources, tools and laws that will go a long way towards creating the spark and catalyst needed to help deliver the promised revolution that will benefit us all. They should also realise the need to respect the opinions of the 'genuine little guys', because it is usually these people who, if protected, will grow into the organisations that will provide millions of much needed jobs in the future. The path of least resistance is not acceptable here.

Our environment and the emergence of the green economy are far too important to be left to the mercy of people who do not deliver what they claim, but who **do** have the resources to threaten anyone who dares to question with defamation law. How can the government of the day promote a green revolution on the one hand, but on the other, fail in every department to protect the very people and organisations that are committed to making it happen?

Chapter 13

For what it's worth

'Sapere aude' ('Dare to be wise').

Horace

Despite the threat of defamation law and complete financial ruin, this book has tried to give an example of the problems associated with the fledgling green economy—an economy that represents the UK's best chance of creating future jobs that provide a better way of life. However, there is no point in complaining about a situation without trying to find an answer to it. The purpose of this final chapter is to put forward a few opinions and suggestions for solutions to some of the problems I have described.

This book is obviously about the waste industry, but the same principles apply to other industries such as solar power and wind power which are still in their infancy. If a solar panels manufacturer is brought into question by a scientist, that manufacturer surely can't be allowed to just run to its lawyer and threaten a law suit. The civilised answer is actually to sit down and discuss the issues raised in the name of scientific progress. Currently, the fledgling solar panel industry is littered with sales sharks that are preying on genuine people to such an extent that the whole of the UK is now sceptical to this ever-advancing technology which is, in fact, a 'no brainer'. The general public's faith and sense of fair play will only be restored when trustworthy brands start to emerge and be protected.

Regarding the waste industry, I hope it is now clear that we need a national policy that is open to challenge by scientists. A good starting point would be the simple diagram below, which shows the UK seeking to maximise the real recycling levels of pure waste commodities that are then traded on the international markets. Converting waste into energy should always be a secondary option, with the minimal residue that's left over going to landfill. Whilst I fully appreciate that 'waste to energy' is a better option than landfill, my opinion is that it should never be marketed as a green economic solution particularly if the waste in the process is exported overseas. Most importantly, this diagram is based on the fundamental principal of transparency and simplicity which everyone can understand.

By maximising the benefits of real recycling, we are maximising the green economy's potential to make the most of waste resources. At the moment there is an unhealthy move, known as the 'dash for ash', towards burning waste that could otherwise be recycled. The problem with burning waste is that it is an easy, lazy option that gets the problem out of the way quickly. However, this waste management technique literally results in the burning of a money making opportunity and produces very few jobs in the green economy. Once a tradable commodity has been burned for energy, it is lost to the economy forever so its value cannot be recycled as an economic multiplier. This point is rammed home on the front cover of this book. The environmental consequences of burning our waste, such as the quality of the air that we breathe, is a question that must be debated by our scientists, along with pressure groups such as Friends of the Earth.

The sad truth is that those involved in the waste industry aren't shouting about the problems of burning waste because of the increased profit margins they are currently making. Burning is currently the best short term financial option for large operators who collect co-mingled waste, as they get a rebate for any fuel source delivered to the furnace. Those who use the real recycling method aren't shouting for change either. This is because the increase in burning for fuel keeps waste commodity prices high for waste streams such as cardboard, paper and plastic. In purely economic terms, it can therefore be argued that the waste industry welcomes the misuse of waste resources as a way to keep the price of tradable commodities high. In my opinion, this is no way to run a green economy as it encourages bad environmental management. This is the reason why the government must step in with clear green policies and laws that are properly communicated and easy to understand. The West's dependence on China as a buyer of our waste commodities, instead of promoting jobs, dealing with waste ourselves and finding secondary markets in the UK, is an economic theory worthy of its own book and one which is an economic and environmental disaster waiting to happen which was only narrowly avoided in the Autumn of 2008.

The one exception to the waste-burning rule is wood. In an earlier chapter, I referred to the UK's fixation on saving trees. The most natural way to have carbon capture is through the growth of sustainable forests, a massive opportunity for creating jobs within the green economy. This is a long term policy that, whilst being pure common sense, is almost non-existent in the UK. A sustainable forest is skilfully managed so that as trees are felled, they are replaced with seedlings on a crop rotation basis. These eventually grow into replacement mature trees. The forest is a working environment that provides wood products for consumer items such as paper and furniture, with the residue being used as biomass fuel. Great care is taken to protect wildlife and to preserve the natural environment at the same time as promoting opportunities in the leisure industry. A sustainable forest works in 30 to 40 year cycles, so one of the main obstacles to overcome here is our culture, which doesn't lend itself to long term planning. You only have to look at Canada, much of Northern Europe and especially Germany to see examples of the opportunity our own green economy is missing out on.

STE Waste has recently had to look at new income streams to ensure its survival, and we came up with the idea of selling sustainable fuels to the growing domestic wood burner market. We have teamed up with English farmers to sell straw-based briquettes, a natural waste product from farms which has an annual carbon neutral cycle. Ironically, I am now, quite literally, a 'man of straw'.

But even in the wood burning industry there are major problems surrounding green markets and, in particular, the phrase *'Wood from a sustainable source'*. How can logs sourced from a forest in Latvia be sustainable for a green economy in the UK, which should ultimately be aiming for environmental autarky, or self sufficiency? The opportunities are endless but they all require commitment and long term planning, which are not currently at the top of the political agenda.

Germany is the best example in Europe of an economy that organises itself and takes a huge interest in environmental concerns and civic pride. Whilst it has certainly had its problems in the last hundred years or so, Germany is a nation that now leads the way regarding quality in manufacturing brands based on long term scientific research and development. There is a window of opportunity for a green revolution in the UK's manufacturing industry, but we need to act on it now before countries like Germany leave us 30 years behind. We need to look to them, emulate them and then find ways of beating them in the competition for global jobs. For the UK, mediocrity is no longer an option if we are to promote a green economy which thrives on trusted products and services that provide a better way.

As an island, we are probably better placed to start a green revolution than anywhere else in Europe—and probably the world. There are two big balls in the sky, one which produces solar power and the other which provides gravitational pull to control the tides, but we have barely started to look at ways of harnessing these power sources to drive our economy. The opportunity is there to secure our freedom and democracy through self sufficiency and the effective management of resources. Not only do we need a national waste policy, but also policies for energy and water supply, and they must all be linked to the green economy.

In my view, the study of our environment should be left to our scientists to debate. And to finish, I would like to point to a historical event which gives a good example of why local spats and discussions like this one are an important part of the bigger picture. One of the remotest places on earth is the Polynesian island of Easter Island. On Easter Sunday 1722, explorers arrived here and found the moai statues, but could find no evidence of who had actually created and erected them.

'*Why Easter Island Collapsed: An Answer for an Enduring Question*' is a detailed essay written by Barzin Pakandam from the Department of Economic History at the London School of Economics. In it, he seeks to shed light on what actually happened on Easter Islands, stating that:

> '*In the past two decades, this continuously growing body of work has arrived at almost unanimous consensus for the existence and symbolic meaning of the statues. The conventional wisdom is grounded in the diligent archaeological work of Jo Anne Van Tilburg (1994), John Flenley (1994, 2003), Paul Bahn (1994, 2003), and further promoted by eco-historians such as Clive Ponting (1991), I.G. Simmons (1989), David Christian (2004), and Jared Diamond (2006). It is a warning to contemporary human civilization: the story of an intelligent and sophisticated society capable of carving, transporting and erecting multi-tonne stone statues by exploiting the natural resources of their island habitat, but eventually collapsing because of the environmental degradation and resource exhaustion that they brought upon themselves*'.

Barzin Pakandam concludes his essay by saying: '*For problems in dealing with Earth's more complex issues pertaining to the environment and human induced climate change, feasible solutions exist. To date what is lacking is cooperation and common understanding. For successful alleviation of modern problems these two attributes must be sought*'.

So the collapse of a sophisticated society due to the mismanagement of resources has happened before—and there is no evidence to suggest it won't happen again if we keep applying *laissez faire* principles to green economics. Scientific principles along with the freedom to collate, discuss and criticise evidence, are the gateway to creating the green economy. The key to its long term success lies in science, together with clearly formed and communicated long term government policy.